DAK SAFETY FILM 5031

1 →1A →2

The SAILBOARD BOOK

BY JAKE GRUBB
WITH SPECIAL CONTRIBUTORS

**THE COMPLETE BOOK OF BOARDSAILING
FROM BEGINNER BASICS
TO WORLD CUP COMPETITION**

A GRUBBSTAKE MEDIA LTD. BOOK

CONTENTS

EDITORIAL, PHOTOGRAPHY, AND DESIGN DIRECTOR: *Jake Grubb*

ART DIRECTOR: *Jim Trumbull*

DESIGN CONSULTANTS: *Mary Mayer, Eileen Abe-Mesias*

ASSISTANT DESIGNER: *Kimberly James*

TECHNICAL EDITOR: *Bruce Matlack*

PROJECT PHOTOGRAPHY: *Jake Grubb, Doug Kaufman, Jim Trumbull*

SPECIAL OPERATIONS: *Julie Schrebe, Darla Reynolds*

LOCATION COORDINATORS: *Craig Spencer, Mary Mayer*

SPECIAL ASSISTANCE: *Reed Lockhart, Jeff Van Horn, Geoff Miller*

COLOR PRODUCTION: *Colormation Inc., El Monte, CA*

LITHOGRAPHY: *Lithocraft Company, Anaheim, CA, Kok Wah Press, Singapore*

TYPOGRAPHY: *Alphabet Type, Tustin, CA*

PHOTOGRAPHIC PRODUCTION: *Colormation Inc., Scott Malcolm, MPS Photographic*

SPECIAL THANKS: *Matlack Windsurfing, San Diego Sailing Centers,*

The Sailboard Book, *by Jake Grubb*

Second Printing

NOTICE: The information in this book is true and complete to the best of our knowledge according to research and data compilation; any recommendations as to equipment choice, equipment modification, or equipment usage are without guarantee by the author and publisher. The Sailboard Book is an independent publication; because design matters, equipment engineering, equipment construction, and individual usage are beyond our control, the author and publisher disclaim any liability incurred in connection with the use of this data or equipment shown and discussed herein.

2 3 4 5 6 7 8 9 0

Printed in Singapore by Kok Wah Press

Library of Congress Catalog Card Number: 84-073077

TO "THE POPE" AND CREW

THE CONTRIBUTORS

BRUCE C. BROWN (pages 149-153, 156, 157, 160-163, 193-199, 203) is a west coast nautical journalist and photographer who has tracked boardsailing's fascinating developments from the shores of Connecticut to the waves of Hawaii. Having published articles internationally on boardsailing, water photography, and yachting competition events of all kinds, Bruce is currently West Coast Editor of the respected Yacht Racing Cruising magazine.

NANCY JOHNSON (pages 100, 104, 105, 108, 115, 120), U.S. women's national champion in the Windsurfer class from 1979 to 1983, is among the finest woman competitors in boardsailing. Well known in the U.S. and abroad, her numerous accomplishments include first place in the 1982 and '83 Mistral North American Championships, first place in the 1982 Mistral World Championships, second place in the 1981 Open Class World Championships, and top woman in the 1982 Pro-Am World Cup. Concentrating on the World Funboard Cup and high performance boardsailing at this writing, Nancy is a respected spokesperson and writer for the sport.

DREW KAMPION (pages 29-37, 39-43), is a veteran writer on boardsailing and surfing topics, noted among peers as the very best at his craft. His descriptive style and penetrating viewpoints are enjoyed monthly in the popular Windsurf magazine where he is Managing Editor.

GUY LEROUX (pages 165-173) is a formidable boardsailing competitor who possesses the rare ability to explain the things that he does just as well as he actually does them. A top-four finisher in seven of ten national and world boardsailing competition events from 1979 to 1983, Guy's excellent magazine articles offer the most lucid explanations of racing skills and tactics available to boardsailing enthusiasts. He is currently completing a book on the subject of sailboard racing.

REED LOCKHART (pages 45-55, 58-73, 132, 141) noted sailmaker and writer on subjects of sailboard technology, looks upon boardsailing's equipment revolution with the eye of a detective and the intensity of a movie critic. Exposed daily to all things "new and better" for the boardsailor, Reed is a no-nonsense purveyor of top quality hardware and proven boardsailor's techniques. His company is a division of Neil Pryde Sails.

BRUCE MATLACK (project technical editor) has been a dedicated boardsailing competitor and businessman for more than a decade. A writer, top notch competitor (first Windsurfer World Champion, two-time North American Champion, numerous other event titles), boardsailing spokesman and merchant, Bruce has been at the center of boardsailing's kaleidoscopic development since the early days of the sport. Currently active in competition, product development, sales and consultation, Bruce is recognized by competitors and allies alike as a serious sailboard purist.

MIKE WALTZE (pages 125-131, 138, 144, 145, 146), sailor, board builder/designer, and author has built a name synonymous with the spectacular in boardsailing. Having first mounted a sailboard while in his early teens, Mike became an adolescent phenomenon, known worldwide for event winning and sailboard exploits always new and seemingly impossible. With a proven groundwork in conventional course racing (multiple titles spanning ten years), Mike is foremost among an elite of performance boardsailing pioneers. Trail blazing such areas as wave riding, wave jumping, and high speed short board sailing, Mike is the personification of boardsailing's ultra-athletes.

CHRIS WILLARD (pages 17-26), a native New Englander transplanted first to the mountains of Utah and then to the waters of Hawaii, is among boardsailing's most descriptive writers. Her words portray the color and fluidity of the sport with a vividness and excitement unmatched. Chris is an established boardsailing competitor, organization participant, merchant, and writer.

Pages 76-77, middle columns, courtesy of Erik Hempel & Wings of Gold Magazine

& thanks to Mary L. Grubb for suggestions and help.

PHOTOGRAPHERS

BRUCE C. BROWN, *widely published marine photographer, is a versatile waterman and journalist. He is West Coast Editor of Yacht Racing Cruising magazine.*

Photo Credits (pages): 20, 22b, 51b, 57, 64bl, 64br, 65b, 68, 97m, 99, 101t, 104b, 110m, 126tr, 127tr, 128r, 130, 132b, 142tr, 143l, 143br, 144, 145br, 145tl, 154, 155, 157tr, 157mr, 161br, 161tl, 162t, 162b, 163tl, 163bl, 171, 173t, 174, 187b, 187t, 196, 199, 200br

PAUL HENGSTEBECK, *a photographer of thirty years experience, began shooting pictures in his native Germany and is an avid recorder of boardsailing as a result of his personal involvement in the sport.*

Photo Credits (pages): 1, 21tr, 22tl, 22tr, 24, 25tr, 25b, 26-27, 33tr, 41br, 47tr, 98bl, 98br, 101b, 112, 117, 151bl, 163tr, 163br, 193tl, 202tr

DAVE EPPERSON, *an outdoor photographer of wide ranging versatility, specializes in boardsailing, bicycling, and all things adventurous. Although based in Southern California, Dave is on mountain or coastal assignment most of the year.*

Photo Credits (pages): front cover, 4-5, 16, 17, 23b, 25tl, 26b, 27b, 37, 48t, 51t, 69t, 74-75, 102m, 107, 109, 115br, 126tl, 129, 131br, 131t, 142tl, 143tr, 145b, 147, 149t, 152, 153t, 153r, 156, 157t, 161ml, 168, 185t, 190, 195t, 208, back cover tr

PAUL KENNEDY, *noted as one of the finest sports photographers in the United States, developed his skills at Sports Illustrated magazine and was one of nine select photographers chosen by the Los Angeles Olympic Committee to document the 1984 Los Angeles Olympic Games. For Paul, boardsailing is a favorite subject.*

Photo Credits (pages): 8-9, 18bl, 21tl, 21br, 31, 96, 97b, 103tr, 104tr, 108tr, 110br, 110-111tm, 118tr, 123t, 146tr, 150, 157b, 164-165, 170b, 179 l, 179b, 198

MARGARET MATLACK *is a boardsailor and photographer who, with her husband Bruce, has chronicled boardsailing since its inception as a sport. Her comprehensive archives show boardsailing in all of its stages in many parts of the world; beautiful pictures that have frozen time in motion.*

Photo Credits (pages): 22tr, 23t, 30tr, 34-35, 98, 100, 102 l, 103br, 108bl, 113, 114, 118tl, 124t, 127b, 151, 153bl, 163tr, 197

GUY MOTIL, *a surfing photographer-turned-boardsailing camera master, captures boardsailing as no other photographer. His unusual views and dramatically lighted subjects show boardsailing in varied and striking dimension. Always unmistakably identifiable, Guy's photographs can be seen in California's Breakout magazine and other publications.*

Photo Credits (pages): 14-15, 18tr, 19, 21tr, 30br, 33b, 36, 42, 43, 44-45, 108tm, 109bl, 119, 122-23, 141tm, 146, 158-59, 179tr, 192-193, 194tr, 200tr, 200ml, 200bl, 201

ADDITIONAL PHOTOGRAPHY

JAKE GRUBB, *12-13, 21b, 28-29, 38-39, 46br, 46 l, 48b, 51m, 56-57, 63b, 64t, 65t, 66, 67, 69b, 71b, 72, 75t, 77r, 78, 79, 80, 81, 82, 83m, 86, 87, 88, 90, 91, 92, 93, 95t, 105, 110tl, 115tr, 116, 124b, 125, 128 l, 132t, 134t, 135t, 137, 166r, 167, 173b, 180m, 180bl, 181tl, 181br, 182r, 183, 184-85, 186, 188, 189, 191, 202b, back cover tr, tl, bl*

DOUG KAUFMAN, *18tl, 39t, 40-41t, 58, 59, 60, 61t, 62t, 63t, 64m, 70, 71, 73, 76, 77 l, 83r, 148-49, 176-77, 180t, 180br, 181m, 182 l, 194tl, back cover br*

JIM TRUMBULL, *46b, 61, 62b, 63m, 84, 85, 170t, 182m, 200tl*

SHARON GREEN, *94-95, 110bl, 166bl, 169, 172, back cover mr*

STEVE WILKINGS, *32, 133, 134b, 135b, 136, 138, 139, 140b, 145m*

MARY MAYER, *166t, 173*

YURI FARRANT, *175*

JEFF FENN *(courtesy UP Sports), 131 l*

JONATHAN WESTON *(courtesy UP Sports), 140t*

TOM KING *(courtesy O'Brien International) 89br*

DAVID BROWNELL *(courtesy Windsurf magazine), 29t, 161r*

HOBIE CAT INC., *206, 51m back cover m*

G.S. SPORTS INC., *30t*

AMF ALCORT INC., *41m, 195b*

WINDSURF MAGAZINE, *52, 97t*

PHOTO CREDIT KEY:

TOP = t, MIDDLE = m, BOTTOM = b, TOP LEFT = tl, TOP MIDDLE = tm, TOP RIGHT = tr, MIDDLE LEFT = ml, MIDDLE RIGHT = mr, BOTTOM LEFT = bl, BOTTOM MIDDLE = bm, BOTTOM RIGHT = br, BACK COVER, FRONT COVER

ACKNOWLEDGEMENTS:

A project such as this, properly done, cannot help but be collaborative to some extent. Boardsailing is broad in scope and growing speedily; producing a book on the subject draws wisdom and insights from a wide range of specialists, some of them athletes, others craftsmen.

First, thanks to Frank Betz, that multi-faceted pioneer who hammered until this book was finally undertaken. Warm appreciation also to: Bruce and Markie Matlack for chronological photos and information, Rick Hoolko and staff at San Diego Sailing Centers for providing sailing and location facilities, Ann Gardner Nelson and Geoff Miller for expert and tireless sailing, Frank McGee and the staff at Colormation Inc. for patient production consultation, Reed Lockhart for diplomatic critique, Jeff Canepa, Rich Jeffries, Steve Murray, Steve Lewis, Paul Collins and Gus Walbolt for encouragement, Brad Thurman and Lithocraft Company for expert printing preparation, and—so

important—Chooch, Dennis Freund, Paul Becker, Cindy Stein, Francois Hilger and the folks at ABI Ltd. who provided more than the means.

The contributors listed on these pages—sailors, competitors, photographers, journalists, and equipment developers, are in each case individualistic—exhibiting style and determination in the things they do best. For this I respectfully thank them. As for the others who lent a comment or a hand along the way, they were appreciated more than they know.

The freshness and energy of boardsailing strikes me every time I see sailor-and-sail breezing across the water. I hope The Sailboard Book brings forth the same wonderful impact to readers each time they pick up this book.

JAKE GRUBB,
NEWPORT BEACH, CALIFORNIA
OCTOBER, 1984

1 SET SAIL

*T*oday is the day. After much mulling and dreaming about whether you could really do it, the opportunity has finally come. Time to head for the beach in search of sun, fun, wind, and of course...that anxious ride on a sailboard!

Departure in the morning sunlight gives way to the roadway bustle of cars, stoplights, exhaust plumes and motor noise. Arrival reveals a different world...cars loaded down with sailboards and paraphernalia, amid expectant folks with smiling faces, young and old. A great day is in the making.

Beach chairs find their places in the sand, sun screen is applied to faces and bodies, and the regulars settle into their patient ritual —waiting for the first breeze of the day. Conversations center around such things as the wind forecast, a new sail design exhibited, someone's first "duck jibe," or the new board a friend just bought.

Then it happens...the first ripples appear on the horizon. Excitement fills the air. Boards are unloaded and the rigging begins. Colorful sails unfold. Booms, masts, and boards are adjoined together one by one and before you know it the chance is ripe for a ride like no other experience. As you enter the water your heart starts beating faster. The sun is

dancing about on the water, creating sparkles that can't sit still. The sky is the deepest of blue, color coordinated with aqua hues of water...so many shades, all soothing to the soul. Tranquility has found you, and the day has just begun!

As you step onto your board, you enter another spectrum, becoming one with the elements. Wind fills your sail as you start a glide across the water. You become driver of an incredible vehicle that's taking you away...to another space, to another place. With wind in your hair and the sun's warmth on your face, cool water splashes you from head to toe. Tasting the cool flavor of rushing water, the crisp scent of air in your nostrils, your senses go into overdrive. All you can do is smile...for you're on top of the world!

This is the sport of sailboarding—the combined forces of wind, water, your rig, and you—all working together to create the sensation of horizontal flight. Each pulsing movement passes through your body, for you are the reason this vehicle is working. Every muscle is being used to hold this sailing craft on course, your reflexes and judgment are going lickity split. Neither time clock nor secretary can catch you now...

HOW TO BEGIN

So is there room in your life for all this? If you're just not sure and need to observe the whole thing, visit a sailboarding regatta. Ask at

any sailboard shop or check with local fleet members for dates and locations. Feel the energy that abounds whenever sailboarders congregate in one spot. The smiles, the laughs, the shared excitement all blend to create a very charged atmosphere. For although sailboarding is an individual sport, it's also quite social if one desires it to be.

Because sailboarding is an experience so readily shared with others you'll usually find a beach full of laughing faces sharing best times and brew at any sailing site. A benefit of this sport is that you can be with friends or completely by yourself, according to mood and preference.

Regattas also offer real challenge for the competitive minded. Your approach can be casual or serious, depending upon desire and personality. Some boardsailors race purely for fun, others prefer to spectate, and still others thrive on the adrenalin of competition. An option is available for everyone; relax and watch, enter for fun, or go for the gold!

SOME WORDS ON BASICS

So once you've made the decision that you must be a part of all this, how and where do you give it the first try? The best way is to start off in a school program, usually offered by your sailboard dealer. Three to five hours of instruction from a competent instructor will save hours of frustration and muscle strain. At the beginning, boardsailing is really a mental sport. You must understand what makes the craft move in different directions, how to tack and jibe, how to use your body most efficiently. Sure, you can figure all this out on your own, but it will generally take much longer—and why waste the time when you can be off sailing so much sooner!

So find a sailboard shop that offers good instruction. It will provide you with a basic foundation and the whole sport will be much less of a mystery. Now don't expect to just sail away without getting wet, because there will be many dunks—that's a guarantee. Falling in the water is part of the game. There will be times when it seems as though you'll never figure this thing out, but don't despair. A little time and perseverance will pay off big when you're suddenly streaking across the water, screaming with glee.

EQUIPMENT NOTES

When first learning to sailboard, you'll want a fairly big board, ten to twelve feet in length. The more stable it is, the easier good balance is achieved. Good balance is the first step to rapid progress. Those beautiful short boards, so popular today, look great but demand real skill. Jumping on to one of these boards too soon will just cause your frustration to multiply, and who needs that?

The size of your sail will depend a lot on the sort of wind your local area gets. You're better off with a sail that's a little too small than one that's too big, so talk to the local sailors—they'll have a good idea as to what's sensible. For sailing in a variety of winds, at least two different sails are advisable—a smaller cut for stronger winds and a larger set-up for lighter winds. As a general rule, single sail owners should opt for a cut slightly on the smaller side. It's better to be a little "under-powered" than "overpowered."

Due to increasing popularity of the sport, used equipment is becoming widely available through dealers and private parties. If your budget says "no way" to new gear, look into the second-hand option. Check bulletin boards at sailboard shops, ask to see the shop's stock, ask fellow sailors and scan the classifieds. Used equipment may not have that "off-the-shelf" shine of a brand new board or sail, but you're on the water...and that's what matters!

Equipment has been a key factor in the development of sailboarding. Colors and styles of boards, sails, and components come in marvelous array. A word to the wise: smart sailors shop with function in mind. Aesthetics and even price are backseat considerations.

CUT LOOSE

You're now into a whole new dimension of life, and needless to say it has much to offer. When daily demands become overwhelming, hopping on a sailboard can provide a rejuvenating escape. Wind and water energize the mind and spirit, while the exertion of boardsailing brings the body a wonderful, vital glow. This is a sport that heats the blood and adds years to life.

Don't be surprised if weather becomes an obsession, wind a compulsive preoccupation, and the afternoon daylight a jewel with no price. For these are the ingredients of a sailboard adventure, and with you and your board the concert begins!

*A*s with most sports, the most visible side of boardsailing is the most explosive, the wildest. We are all quite naturally drawn to novelty, to extremes, to the biggest and the best. And so the media is full of the most outrageous and advanced forms of boardsailing; from sailing on giant Hawaiian waves and launching fifty-foot jumps, to flat-out speed runs in forty-knot gales. The danger and precariousness of boardsailing is often brought into the foreground of the public consciousness, and many who might be interested pass on the opportunity to learn to windsurf.

The truth is that boardsailing is quite accessible to almost anyone, anywhere...at any age...at virtually any level of physical ability. Wherever there's a breeze and water— be it a pond, a lake, a reservoir, a bay, an ocean—there can be boardsailing. Board-sailing is a very social, but also a highly individual activity. It's easy to learn, available to all, and it opens the door to a lifetime of growing adventure.

FREESAIL ORIGINS

The "Windsurfer®" grew out of a meeting of minds. The minds belonged to Jim Drake, a Southern California sailor and aeronautical

Far Left: Aeronautical engineer James Drake, co-developer of the first modern sailboard incorporating the "freesail system" as we know it. Left: Hoyle Schweitzer, co-developer of the modern sailboard and founder of Windsurfer®, the first sailboard manufacturer.

engineer, and Hoyle Schweitzer, a Southern California surfer and computer executive. Somehow they decided to combine their two sports—put a sail on a surfboard—and that's basically what they did. It sounds simple, but actually there were a number of technical wrinkles to iron out; by the time they did, they had developed quite a sophisticated little gizmo. Sophisticated and different enough that they applied for, and received, a patent on their new apparatus.

The three chief components that made the product unique were its universal joint, wishbone boom, and sail shape. The "universal" connects the mast to the board, creating a fully articulated rig. This means that the sailor can allow the mast to fall and the board will remain upright, a great convenience for the novice. The wishbone boom gives the sailor something to hold onto and with which to control the position of the sail. Its wishbone shape means that it can be sailed from either the port or the starboard side of the sail. The sail itself is a logical solution to the relationship between the mast and the wishbone boom, being essentially triangular in shape and having a prominent clear "window" through which to

see what's going on "over there." Another great convenience—for novice and expert alike.

Although invented in California, the Windsurfer failed to catch on there at first; it wasn't until the boards were taken to Europe that things began to take off. Glenn Taylor, an early boardsailing dealer and author, visited Europe in the early 1970's and brought some sailboards along. His wife Kristine relates: "People actually jumped off of bridges in their clothes to ask Glenn where they could get

a sailboard!" Today Glenn and Kristine operate Bay Windsurfing, near San Francisco, where their weekly regattas, evening sails, lessons and social gatherings have created a real boardsailing energy center.

"The social thing is a big deal," Glenn Taylor says. "It's the guts of the experience. The sport didn't start out to make money; it was just people getting together that shared this interest. As with any sport, the professional competitors are in it to make money, and manufacturers must earn a profit, but

the thing that keeps people coming back is social."

Certainly it is the social side that gives boardsailing its broad scope. The phenomenal growth of the sport in Europe (sales from 1979 to 1984 exceeded 1.5 million boards) has been nourished by countless boardsailing shops with their clubs and instruction courses, their endless parties and regattas. In fact, freesail fever grew so contagious that soon it was spreading like wildfire, world-wide; and it was spreading in some surprising directions.

PROLIFERATION

It started in Holland, swept into Germany and France, then spilled out into Scandanavia, Switzerland and Italy, England and Ireland, the Soviet Union and Israel, South Africa and Canada, Hawaii and Japan, Australia and Florida, Brazil and California. Soon it was nearly everywhere, accessible to almost anyone. Even Cuba, where the people are not allowed the hazard of freedom to sail, fielded a specially taught boardsailing team at the '83 Pan American Games in Caracus.

But this isn't all. As if the breezes on the summertime oceans and lakes weren't sufficient—and they aren't—the alternative applications began to arise: skate sailing, ice boarding, wind skiing, skateboard sailing, speed sailing, roller sailing, and who knows how many more applications of the ingenious freesail system have been translated into vehicles that transported devotees at good speed across desert, ice, snow and pavement? Suffice to say that the freesail system has opened enormous recreational opportunities worldwide.

HOW IT WORKS

Like every sailor, a boardsailor rides the wind. The sail of his board is a vertical wing that is actually *drawn into* the wind more than it is pushed by it (such are the marvelously strange laws of physics). The boardsailor is the balancing point at the center of a number of forces: the force of the wind, the weight of the sailboard, the weight of the rig, the lift of the sail, and the resistance of the daggerboard or fins. Indeed, the physics of boardsailing is significantly more complicated than the physics of conventional boat sailing because in boardsailing the sailor actually becomes an integral part of the relationship between board and sail. This is why the sensations are so great in freesailing.

Yet, despite the fact that physicists and mathematicians might be hard-pressed to sort out all the vectors and factors at work in an average moment of boardsailing, it's really quite simple from the point-of-view

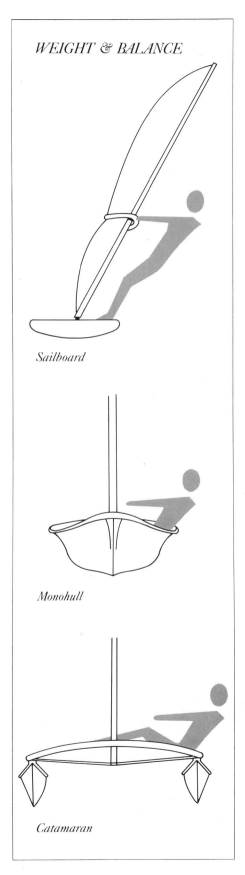

Sailboard

Monohull

Catamaran

of the sailor: you just lean back until your weight or strength balances the force of the wind's effect on the sail. You transmit what's left over through your feet into the board. The result is forward motion! You can ease off the pressure by luffing the sail; you can increase it by doing the reverse (sheeting in). You can fine-tune your course and turn by moving the sail forward or aft and from one side to the other, thereby changing its "center of effort." In short, you can go anywhere you want to go simply by making subtle adjustments to the forces available.

On a conventional boat, the force of the wind heels the craft to leeward. On a sailboard, the sailor balances the force of the wind by heeling to windward. In either case, as the wind increases, the angle increases. But with a conventional boat, the force of the wind is pressing the sailboat deeper into the water and heeling it over onto its side. With a sailboard, the

BOARDS & BASICS

force of the wind is creating lift, the hull stays flat on the water and the board starts to "fly." This is one reason the sailboard is virtually the fastest kind of sailboat in the world.

Whereas the explanation of the forces at work in boardsailing might be quite complicated, the experience is quite simple, though rich. The native intelligence of the human body and mind can understand all these converging factors in a short time; and, while the mathematician is still working away on his calculations, the boardsailor can simply lean back into the wind and sail away in a natural balancing of forces.

CLASSIFICATIONS

Where once there was only the original, basic Windsurfer, there are now several classifications of sailboard, each with their own competitions, ideal wind and water conditions, specialized equipment and superstars.

There is Open Class, including Division I (flat-bottomed production boards) and Division II (round-bottomed production boards); there are the One-Design classes, in which identical boards from the same manufacturer (like Windsurfer, Mistral, Windglider and Wayler) compete in various disciplines; there is Construction Class, where high-performance high-tech boards compete in World Cup competition; there is Surfsailing, in which the sport really

comes closest to the word "wind-surfing" and for which the boards are generally smaller, lighter and more maneuverable, like surfboards.

Significant advancements in each of these areas, both in equipment and skill level, has created a world-wide community of competitive boardsailors, some professional, some amateur, but all ultimately involved for the lifestyle, that effervescent brew of freewheeling fun, a sense of pioneering new personal frontiers, and the unlimited possibilities for satisfying common-interest friendships.

YOU VS. YOU

Perhaps the real beauty of board-sailing is the fine personal challenge it offers—for both young and old—in the invigorating natural environment of wind and water. Bert Salisbury of Seattle, Hoyle Schweitzer's first paying customer, comments: "There are many things you can do that require putting in a lot of effort to

get a short, peak experience. You spend high energy to climb a mountain for those few seconds on the top. But I've had a lot of peak experiences on a sailboard. Like sailing at night in high winds, or having schools of fish or whales break the surface all around you."

Once, sailing island-to-island in the Puget Sound, Bert encountered grey whales in the Saratoga Channel. "At first I thought it was a nuclear submarine," he recalls, "and then I saw the huge tail of one of them, and they came up all around me. Enormous beasts, surging by, and me on a little chip!" Now, Bert says, "I've given up racing in all respects. I'm into the broader experience of boardsailing."

At the extreme end of the self-challenging side of the sport are sailors like Arnaud de Rosnay, a French baron, former backgammon champion and the first man to sail across the North African desert with a freesail system (mounted

on the Speed Sail he invented). De Rosnay is continually challenging himself and his boardsailing abilities, and has built himself into a significant international media phenomenon, with crossings of the Bering Straight (USA to USSR), Gibraltar, the English Channel, the Gulf Stream (Florida to Havana) and a 700-mile life-or-death crossing between South Pacific islands. He lives in Maui, which has become the world center of surfsailing, where he trains on the powerful waves of Hookipa for more testing of his personal limits.

IT TAKES ALL KINDS

Just as abilities cover a broad spectrum, so—fortunately—do sites and conditions. By selecting the correct place and time to board-sail, each person is headed for a rewarding and enjoyable experience. A novice doesn't set off from Maalaea, Maui, in 25-knot offshore winds; not on your life! A novice finds a nice, small, closed-in body of water with 360° access. In time (sooner than later), a more challenging spot with a brisker wind will seem alluring.

It all starts with a simple, humble beginning, but what great thing doesn't? The simple task of listening attentively to an instructor, following his recommendations, and not being afraid of getting a little embarrassed—and more than a little wet—will lead to places now inaccessible.

Every year thousands learn to boardsail, working their way through all the little tests—of balance, of technique, of knowledge of wind and weather and equipment, of danger and safety. And each test is followed by a graduation, a "peak experience," a taste of emerging freedom and the appetite for more of the freesail experience.

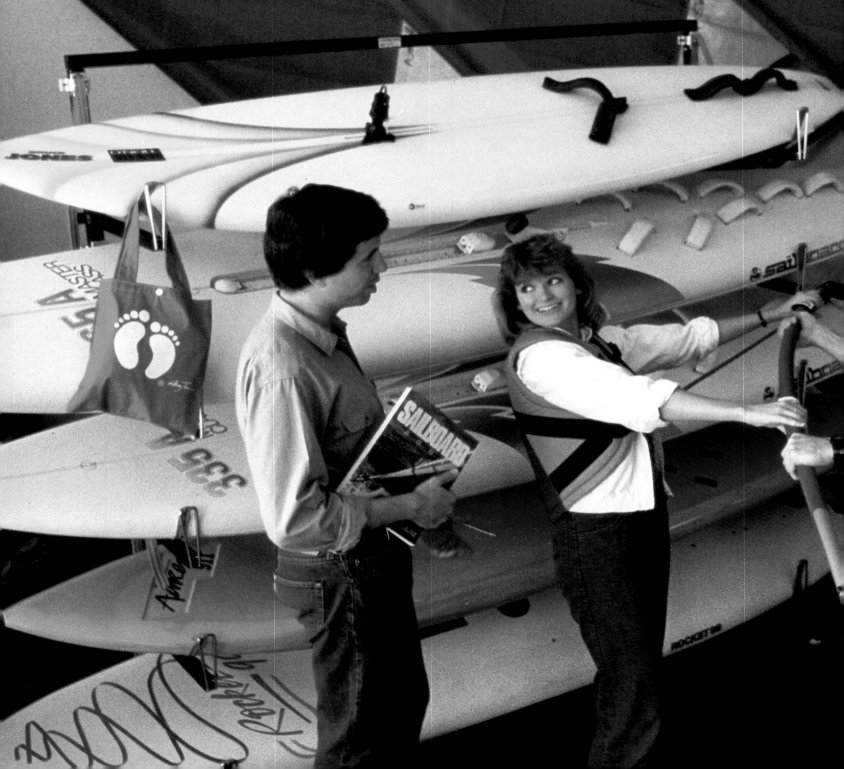

3 THE BEST BOARD FOR YOU

*N*o matter how much you've heard about boardsailing, or seen it happening on the lakes and bays around you, or have dreamt about doing it, the experience of entering a boardsailing retail establishment can still be mind-boggling.

In an instant, entering a "shop" can bring you face to face with techno-shock—that sense of being struck in the brain with everything you were always afraid you were supposed to know, so you didn't ask. Indeed, the array of hulls, sails, booms, masts, centerboards, fins, mast tracks and paraphernalia—not to mention salespersons—can be a strong inducement to re-route your best intentions right out the door again.

But, stay! All is not lost. Honest.

Despite the proliferation of sailboard designs and models, selecting the right board for yourself is a relatively simple task. Unless you're an absolute fanatic for technical flagellation, some general descriptions and guidelines will most likely be sufficient to put you on the right board.

CLASSIFICATIONS

As discussed in the last chapter, several distinct categories of sailboard have emerged, all in a logical progression. Still newer developments are emerging or are yet to come. But for the present, we can talk about the four major classifications of sailboards:

Division I: The first Division I was the Windsurfer, and it continues as the number one in popularity worldwide, although most other manufacturers now also produce Division I sailboards. These boards are characterized by flat-bottomed hulls, daggerboards, large volume, lack of footstraps (though they can be an option) and basic surfboard-like curves and outlines.

Division II: Division II is what happened to boards when Europeans entered sailboarding and brought forth a different influence. The evolutionary line here is yachting, not surfing. These boards have very rounded hulls; they're quite thick, especially in the bow, and generally have an even greater volume than Division I boards.

Funboards: This is a term that defies classification and/or definition, yet it's used. (What sailboard *isn't* fun?) What it loosely describes is a new generation of sailboard that occupies the high-performance end of the equipment spectrum. Funboard hulls integrate elements from Division I boards, Division II boards, and modern surfboards. (Division I boards draw on earlier surfboard know-how.) The original prototype funboards, called Pan Am boards after the Pan Am Windsurfing World Cup in which they were first popularized, are generally longer and narrower than Division I boards, with a rounded bottom in the bow reminiscent of a Division II hull—though less extreme. Amidships, they are flat bottomed, like Division I; but in the stern they are narrow and thin, like modern big-wave surfboards.

Modern Funboards, like their Pan Am parents, feature footstraps

(to keep rider and board together in high winds, heavy seas, and on waves), a retractable centerboard and, recently, a sliding mast track that allows the mast to move forward for up-wind sailing and back for downwind sailing.

Consumer funboards are generally shorter than stock Division I and also lengthier Pan Am boards. Today there are a wide range of variations on the funboard idea, including slalom boards, course racing boards and the open ocean boards.

Wave Boards: These are funboards for the waves—essentially surfboards with added volume to accommodate the extra weight of the rig and standing rider. Wave boards have only fins, no centerboard; they have footstraps and an adjustable mast track, though because of the low volume and sensitivity of these boards, the mast is positioned on the beach to suit existing conditions. Wave boards are also sometimes called jump boards, because most are used for wave jumping as well as wave riding. Purists sometimes have special boards for wave riding and special boards for wave jumping.

NATURAL SELECTION

Historically speaking, most folks learn to sail on *Division I boards*. They're stable, floaty, forgiving, simple, and most of them perform well on all points of sail. Many models boast huge international class racing associations. The boards are usually molded out of polyethylene or alternate durable foam-filled plastic materials, so they're rugged and easy to care for.

For the beginning sailor, any major Division I one-design board is a no-fault starting point; however, because of the great competitive and social structures that have grown up around these sailboards, many sailors stay with a certain brand as

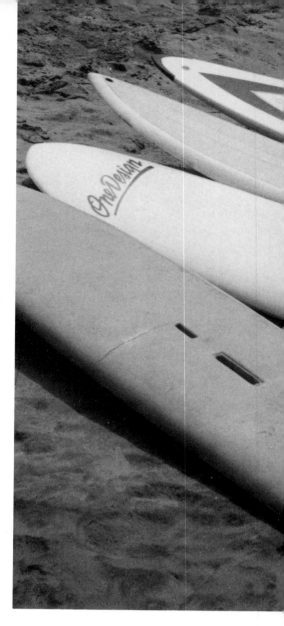

Division I Board

Variety of sailboards pictured includes: (left to right) Original One-Design production Windsurfer, modern One-Design production Windsurfer, early Pan Am World Cup "funboard," modern World Cup type funboard, early custom wave board, modern production wave board, and modern custom wave board.

Division II Board

Fun Board

Wave Board

DIFFERENT BOARDS, DIFFERENT FUNCTIONS

their experience grows. These boards will accommodate the evolving abilities of the sailor throughout his/her growth.

Division II boards are great in light winds, and they're terrific going to weather, but they're frustratingly difficult off the wind—or at any point of sail for the novice. These are generally high-tech, expensive boards that appeal to the true technocrat. They're great to try once you've mastered the flat-bottomed boards, but not before. Like Division I, they're often made of molded plastic, though many are one-offs of foam and exotic resins and cloth.

It is beginning to be said that future sailors will learn to boardsail on funboards, progress on funboards, and reach the top on funboards. This could well be true, except for some micro-hitches with these racer/cruisers. Though more and more companies are manufacturing funboards using various molding techniques, many are handmade "custom" models of foam and assorted glass shells, most beautiful but brittle. They're also built for good winds: the thin, narrow tails

Modern sailboards come in many types and employ several construction processes, including ABS, ASA, Polyethylene, and fiberglass. ABS is the most inexpensive mass production process, consisting of a polyurethane foam inner core protected by a hard outer shell which is pressed together in top and bottom halves. ASA is similar to ABS, but incorporates special additives for more durability and sunlight protection. This process also features a reinforced "welded" seam. Polyethylene is yet another method, and is either "blow-molded" or "roto-molded." Each of these processes offers seamless skinning. Roto-molding, being noted as the best and most expensive of the two polyethylene applications, enables non-skid top surfacing while in production, skin thickness control in the rail sections, and has a smoother bottom finish. Custom performance boards (at right) are handmade from polyurethane foam and skinned with lightweight fiberglass. They're marvelous but easily damaged. New mass production methods, such as epoxy amalgums, are achieving growing popularity.

sink in anything under 15 knots. The narrow outline, low volume, "drawn-out" lines, the flat bottom "rocker;" these and more make the standard funboard a bit frustrating in light air. They're definitely for the sailor who's willing to wait for the wind or who will go chase after it.

Wave boards, of course, are for the advanced. They must be water-started, and that means fairly strong breezes are required. Almost all are custom shaped out of foam and are covered with one of various resin/cloth combinations. The wave/jump board definitely has its applications and is not out of place anywhere there's water, as long as there's a good amount of wind.

For the beginning boardsailor in most locations, the flat-bottomed Division I boards are the logical beginning. From there on, while you probably want to keep that board around; it's a matter of philosophic choice whether to move in the direction of round-bottom boards or funboards (and through funboards on to surfsailing with wave boards). The round bottom board appeals more to the technician and the strategist, perhaps. The funboard lures the sailor who wants to go fast and get radical. Each is limited by the realities of the weather and geography, yet each has its days.

As a beginning boardsailor, once you have lessons and can get where you want to go on a body of water, you'll find yourself out among other sailors on other kinds of boards. Take the opportunity to try as many boards as possible, because ultimately sailboard selection is a function not of the mind and its theories, but of the body and its individual kinesthetics.

4 SAILS, MASTS & COMPONENTS

*T*he next time you go sailboarding in moderate to windy conditions, pick out a couple of the hottest sailors and watch them tune their sails before launching....concentration, attention to detail, a purpose for every adjustment. This is the mark of a sailor who gets the very most out of his rig.

The sail is, of course, the sailor's powerplant, and understanding how to "tune" it is essential to getting the best results from both equipment and sailing conditions.

HOW SAILS WORK...& WHY

Man used sails for centuries before understanding the basic principles which make them function. For this understanding, we can thank Daniel Bernoulli, who in 1738 discovered the wonders of fluid flow. With a foil shaped sail, Bernoulli's findings show that when moving through air there is a pressure build-up on the windward side which exceeds the pressure on the outer (convex) side of the sail. This phenomenon of physics results in a pulling or "sucking" effect, which in the case of a sailing craft makes the craft move! When this force on the sail is combined with the "lateral resistance" generated from the daggerboard and skeg on a sailboard, the path of least resistance is forward—as opposed

HOW SAILS WORK

to sideways. Thus, the venting of these two forces results in forward motion.

So, off we go at, say, a 45 degree angle to the true wind. We're taking advantage of the laws of physics to zip along in fast fun and high style. And as if that's not enough,

the board and rig make their own wind while in motion, further increasing the speed of your sailboard! Just as you feel a breeze when bicycling even on a calm day, so does the sail "see" or "feel" not only the true wind that's blowing, but also the "apparent" wind created by board and sail as they move over water. The result is performance—and that heady sense of freedom that you feel when a sailboard gets moving.

SAIL TERMS AND OBJECTIVES

There's probably nothing duller than memorizing nautical lingo—especially sail terminology...until it means something. Getting the draft forward and the leech properly tensioned are playful word games at best until you know what folks are talking about. All this begins to make sense when the sail comes out of the bag, you hang it on the mast and try to give it a desirable shape. Terms and objectives begin to come clear and tuning the sail becomes a purposeful exercise rather than a frustrating puzzle.

Several factors contribute to a sail's shape—some of them inherent in the sail's "cut" and others relating to a sailor's skill in rigging and

"tuning" his sail. These include: 1) luff curve shape, 2) seam taper (the curve built into the sail's seams), 3) cloth stretch (or resistance to stretch) 4) and adjustment or "trim." Because items 1 through 3 above are matters controlled by the sailmaker, we'll concentrate on item 4, adjustment. While the sailmaker builds "draft" or pocket into a sail, you as a sailor determine the specific adjustment and shape refinement.

"Draft" is the amount of curve in the sail at its fullest area, and also the location of that fullest area. The draft or "pocket" can be moved vertically and horizontally. The amount of draft in a sail depends upon the specific type of sail and how it is adjusted for a given set of weather conditions. A well used stock regatta sail, for example, would tend to have considerably more draft in its inherent shape than a very small, mylar full batten wave board sail that's right off the shelf.

Just as a sail produces power as a result of its curved shape, the specific characteristics of that shape account for the differences in the way sails perform. Not all sails look the same, not all sails are used for the same thing, and not all sails perform the same.

Excellent view of sail "draft" can be seen in this overhead photograph of a boardsailor cruising along on reach

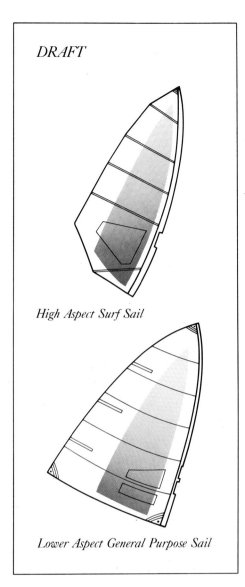

DRAFT

High Aspect Surf Sail

Lower Aspect General Purpose Sail

Excessive "leech twist" in sail at left allows air to "spill" from the sail, reducing power.

Generally, a fuller, deeper sail will produce more power and greater speed on a reach—especially at light to moderate wind velocities—than a flatter sail of similiar shape. The flatter sail will usually allow a board to "point" higher into the wind, and it will be easier for a sailor to control—especially at higher speeds in waves and stronger winds.

So a sail is made for a purpose. And it has a basic "cut" which gives it a certain amount of draft. The position of the draft is critical to getting proper performance from the sail. You, the sailor, determine draft position through the adjust-ments you make when setting up the sail for a day on the water.

DRAFT POSITION

There has been, is now, and always will be much debate over the nuances of sail shape and draft position among sailboarding experts. But most agree on some principles.

Essentially, a boardsail's draft should not be too far behind the mast. That is, the point of deepest pocket in the sail should not be excessively far back toward the leech of the sail. The matter of exactly how far back is too far could reduce many sailmakers to a state of intoxicated belligerence if the question were raised at a pizza joint after a race! But it's safe to say that no boardsail should have its point of maximum fullness built in aft of the mid-point between mast and clew. Within this parameter, different types of rigs incorporate different optimum draft positions. But the "mid-point" limit is a guideline to go by.

Vertical draft position is just as important. The general rule here is that the top or head of the sail should be flatter than the middle and lower sections. This is especially true in windy or gusty conditions where too much power at the top of the sail can be too tough to handle, pitching you unceremoniously head first over the nose of the board. Worse, a sail head that's too full can actually turn inside out when you luff or depower in a wind puff. The result here is a quick backside splash in the water. Less fun for you than your jeering friends on the beach!

LEECH TWIST

Though difficult to describe, "leech twist" is a phenomenon that affects sail performance significantly. It can be seen when the leech, or trailing edge of the sail, takes on a sort of curl in a direction away from the wind. This "leech fall-off," which is usually most noticeable in the upper sections of the sail, is desirable and necessary in small, controlled doses. But many boardsails have too much of it, resulting in a "floppy" appearance at the top, poor wind-ward performance, and excessive aerodynamic drag. There are four ways to deal with this: 1) carefully doublecheck and re-adjust the out-

THE MAGIC TERM: "ASPECT RATIO"

Modern "high aspect" sail

haul, 2) purchase a stiffer mast, 3) purchase a better quality sail, 4) just plain live with the imperfection. Like so many things, this is a matter of personal assessment.

ASPECT RATIO

Three "buzzwords" often found in boardsail conversation are "high aspect ratio." These words, when applied to a sail, have been known to imbue it with mystic power which enables the user to perform supernatural feats! Actually, a high aspect ratio sail (H.A.R.) is simply a sail which is tall and skinny compared to a more traditional low aspect ratio sail, which has a more standard triangular look.

While aspect ratio is technically a sail's luff length squared, divided by its area, marketing people have used the term "high aspect ratio" as though to describe something exotic beyond the realm of normal calculation. H.A.R. is just one of many design concepts—something that has proved effective for certain applications in sailboarding. In surfsailing, for example, shorter booms give sailors more freedom to perform. High aspect ratio sails fit on short booms.

But IYRU rules still require longer, more conventional booms on Division I and Division II boards for competition. Thus, most standard boards do not incorporate and in fact do not need high aspect ratio sails. But with funboards for both recreation

Modern recreational/regatta sails

and competition, the trend is toward high aspect ratio sails, as the influence here is surfsailing and World Cup racing.

So, because of their short booms, controllability, and overall handling ease, high aspect ratio sails are appealing. But from a consumer standpoint, don't fall victim to the notion that a sail with an aspect ratio of 3.41 is necessarily better than one with a 3.38 ratio. End performance is a composite of several factors.

THE SAILBOARD & RIG

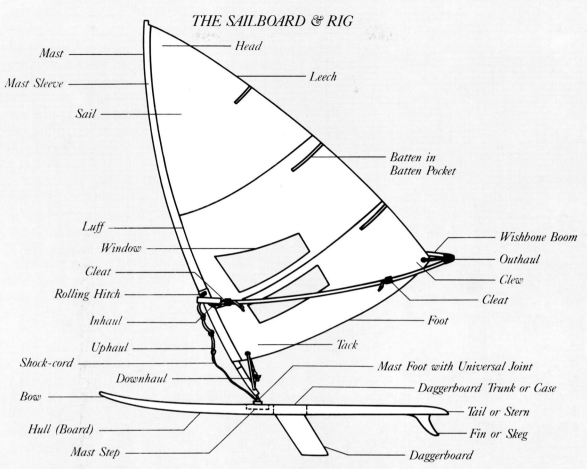

Mast — Head
Mast Sleeve — Leech
Sail
Batten in Batten Pocket
Luff — Wishbone Boom
Window — Outhaul
Cleat — Clew
Rolling Hitch — Cleat
Inhaul — Foot
Uphaul — Tack
Shock-cord — Mast Foot with Universal Joint
Downhaul — Daggerboard Trunk or Case
Bow — Tail or Stern
Hull (Board) — Fin or Skeg
Mast Step — Daggerboard

SAIL ASPECT RATIO

$AR = S^2 \div A$ Aspect Ratio = Span Squared ÷ Area
(Luff Length)

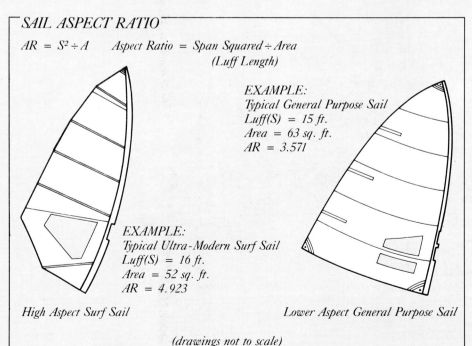

EXAMPLE:
Typical General Purpose Sail
Luff(S) = 15 ft.
Area = 63 sq. ft.
AR = 3.571

EXAMPLE:
Typical Ultra-Modern Surf Sail
Luff(S) = 16 ft.
Area = 52 sq. ft.
AR = 4.923

High Aspect Surf Sail

Lower Aspect General Purpose Sail

(drawings not to scale)

SAILBOARD COMPONENTS

Hull—High flotation "board" specially designed and crafted to allow sailor stand-up sail control

Sail—Wind harnessing device, specially designed and crafted from dacron, mylar, or other modern lightweight cloth substances

Mast—The pole or "spar" which supports the sail vertically

Boom—The tubular bars or "spars" which support the sail horizontally; these are a "wishbone" configuration with front end attaching to the mast and rear end attaching to the sail's "clew" or rear-most corner.

Mast Base—The tube or cup which fits into the mast and attaches to the specific mechanism which allows the rig its free movement.

Universal—The device, fitted between mast base and board, which permits the mast to move freely

Mast Foot—The coupler or part which attaches the universal to the board

SAIL TYPES & FUNCTIONS

TYPES OF SAILS

It's blowing 14 knots, the sun is shining, the water is lively but not rough, and you're on the beach observing the action. Due to the conditions, almost every type of rig imaginable is out and about. And what an assortment of different looking sails! Some have no battens, some have battens across the whole width of the sail. Some have clews that seem to be at the sail's head height. Some are made of bright colored dacron, yet several are cut from a translucent "mylar" film material. Many appear baggy in contour, while others are taut—almost flat. Why so much variation?

The answer is that our 14-knot day—a typical healthy wind velocity at many a boardsailing spot—provides conditions which permit a large variety of sail types to function. Some, however, are better suited to the conditions than others. Let's take a closer look.

REGATTA SAILS

In common lingo, regatta sails are those which are used for conventional triangle racing, encompassing International Divison I, Division II, and One Design classes. In the familiar Windsurfer class, for example, sails must conform to a configuration characterized by three battens, an 8-ft. 6-inch boom, a 14-ft. 2-inch mast, and a specific leech length. This brings about a low aspect, triangular-looking sail. Since much regatta competition is done in light to moderate winds, sails such as these are usually cut fairly full; they offer excellent versatility. Most new "standard" sailboards are sold with sails of this basic type. Though their performance in strong winds and rough conditions is not the best, they function well all-around.

FUNBOARD SAILS

These are sails built upon the influence of World Cup sailboard racing. Their design, largely for higher wind, fast open water racing, is unregulated by any class or manufacturer's rules. Funboard sail design is the proving ground for many innovative ideas.

Initially, surf sail design influenced World Cup type sails, but as surf-sailing boards have become shorter and funboards more specialized, their corresponding sails have differed also. Classic World Cup type sails are cut for booms 6 to 18-inches longer than surf sail booms, and they're designed to be used on very stiff aluminum or carbon-graphite masts. These sails must have higher clews than traditional regatta sails, to prevent booms from dragging during high speed reaches where the mast is raked radically aft.

At this writing, most funboard sails are higher aspect than regatta sails, but lower aspect than surf sails. They are generally flatter than regatta sails, although some schools tend toward a bit more fullness for more power. A common funboard sail "plan form" dictates 3-5 battens, supporting a moderate amount of roach. Innovations seem limitless, including extra wide mast socks which help to reduce air turbulence around the mast, full batten sail designs, and even extra wide "wing" mast experiments for super aerodynamic efficiency.

Full race World Cup sails are made from many different kinds of materials, among them specially resinated ultra weave dacrons and super exotic mylar/Kevlar composites. Just as these materials are excellent for high speed no-holds-barred racing, their less esoteric mass market versions do a great job of powering funboards of all kinds.

SURF SAILS

Although they may not be the most useful for typical lake or bay sailing, surf sails certainly get the biggest share of media coverage. Surf sails are an integral part of boardsailing's performance evolution—that pioneer cutting edge of the sport where ocean waves are so often a test bed.

For our purposes we'll consider that surf sails are those sails which have evolved for use in the surf—but which are also used in flat water on the shorter style (under 10-ft.) sailboards. Although a good surf sail ought to supply adequate speed, power, and windward effectiveness, the real premium with this type of sail is control.

The great appeal of shorter boards lies in the freedom to execute quick turns, jibes, and jumps. It is the primary function of a surf sail to allow the rider maximum maneuverability while maintaining planing speed. Since short boards will not work very well in wind velocities below 15 mph, their sails are generally not cut to accommodate light wind performance. As such they are quite flat. This flatness is effective for several reasons. First, flatter sails are easier to control in a stiff breeze. And flatter sails with flat head sections are comparatively forgiving in wind puffs—yet they are responsive.

Now think back to the description of "apparent wind"—that wind which the board and rig create as

Standard sails are excellent for all-around boardsailing.

Funboard sail is usually "higher aspect," thus more streamlined than a standard recreational sail.

Surfsailors utilize special "high aspect" surf sails

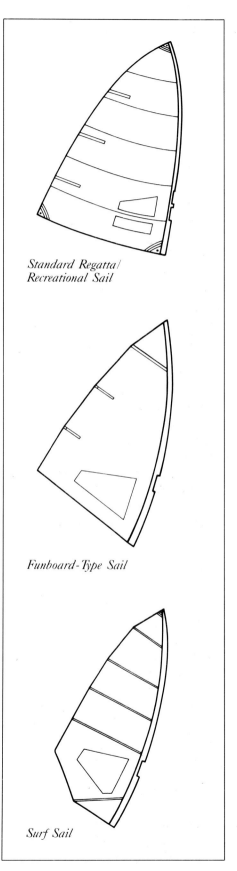

Standard Regatta/ Recreational Sail

Funboard-Type Sail

Surf Sail

a result of forward movement. Imagine, at this point, that you are sailing toward the beach on a big-surf day at famous Hookipa, Maui. It's blowing 25 knots and you're really screaming along, almost overpowered. Board speed is 15-knots. Suddenly you spot a 10-ft. high wave. You decide that if you can just get your knees to stop shaking you're going to try to ride that wave! You line up, bear off slightly and start accelerating down the face of the wave. Before you even reach the bottom of the wave you've accelerated to a burst of 25-knots—35-knots with your apparent wind! As if all this isn't wild enough, right now is when you want to power that downwind right turn and shoot back up to the crest of the wave in prepara-

tion for another dash down the wave's face!

The foregoing has been an attempt to illustrate that if you don't have a flat, easy-to-handle sail with a short boom when in the waves, you're better off at home watching the soap operas!

Obviously, not all sails used on short boards will undergo the extreme conditions described here. While a Hookipa (Maui) regular may use a 50-square foot sail with full battens and 5-ft. 6-inch booms, a high wind lake sailor may prefer a 50-square foot sail with one full batten, two partial battens, and a 6-ft., 6-inch boom assembly. The point here is that surf sails should be cut flat and preferably have battens. They should be fitted to short booms and

they need to be built strong to withstand the rigors of surf and high wind use.

Surf sails are usually cut for medium-stiff masts—those stiff enough for good sail shape but supple enough to survive crashes in the waves. In order to provide stability and minimize leech twist, these sails commonly have a lot of curve cut into the luff. The high loads which result from the extreme sail tensions and rough treatment are often countered by the use of very firm dacron cloths and mylar fabrics. Often in two or even three layers, these "plys" are reinforced along areas of high load such as the leech and foot. New techniques for strength and lightness are under continuous experimentation.

SAILBOARD MASTS AND COMPONENTS

Suppose for a moment that you've suddenly become the world's most knowledgeable boardsailor, and that you're equipped with the world's best boardsails. The sum total of all your knowledge, all the sailmaker's design insight and craftsmanship, combined with the greatest sailing skill and sail trimming ability—all these elements cannot extract top performance from your sails if you're not using the proper components. Masts, booms, and mast-to-board couplings must all function in harmony with the sail, rider, and board. This is essential if the sail's design potential (and resultant fun) are to be achieved.

First time sailboard buyers are commonly flabbergasted by the wide variety of masts, booms, and mast bases offered by manufacturers. This frustration is entirely understandable, since rapid development of the sport has promoted both the quick obsolescence of parts, and the proliferation of suppliers. The rate of change is such that even dealers and "experts" find it tough to stay on top of all the newest developments. Shown here are charts which describe some of the most common types of components. When analyzing the information on these charts, keep in mind: 1) the great variety of products available make it impossible to offer a complete, up-to-the-second component catalogue; the information here is intended only as a guide that can help you evaluate a large segment of the gear available. 2) components often achieve very different working results from one another. A soft, lightweight fiberglass mast which might be an ideal recreational mast for the novice will make a poor surf or racing mast—and vice versa.

be realistic about your needs before deciding on any new gear.

SAILBOARD COMPONENTS GUIDE

GUIDE TO SAILBOARD MASTS

Type	Advantages	Disadvantages
Soft (quite flexible), (epoxy fiberglass construction) Example: Windsurfer	Lightweight, modest price, forgiving (good for high wind beginners), often the only legal mast in One Design classes.	Will not support good sail shape, especially in high wind or with high aspect ratio or "plump-head" sails. Often fairly easy to break under load.
Stiff fiberglass (usually epoxy) construction Examples: Ampro, Windsurfer Rocket, Tubes X	Moderately good sail shape retention (with properly designed sails), easily extendable for taller sails, generally strong enough for surf, high wind.	Relatively heavy, optimum stiffness not achievable due to weight and materials considerations.
Aluminum alloy Examples: North, Neil Pryde, Serfiac	Good sail shape retention, stiff, well suited to regatta and funboard racing.	Most brands not strong enough for high-stress (e.g. surf) use. Better brands more expensive than fiberglass masts. Lesser brands liable to permanent bend under high load. Most should not be used with mast extensions.
Carbon fiber reinforced epoxy-fiberglass Examples: Ampro, Concept II	Very stiff (allows good sail shape), generally good stiffness-to-weight ratio.	Quite expensive, usually too brittle for surf use, not legal for some class racing.
Multiple piece masts Examples: Ampro, F2	Convenient, practical to repair because if broken the breakage tends to be in one piece only.	Sometimes difficult to disassemble, expensive.
Wing Mast Example: Dimitrije Milovich's world record setter, utilized on special Sailboards Maui speed board	Over-rotating, foiled leading edge offers superior performance; oriented toward speed trials and World Cup racing.	Not (at this writing) yet thoroughly tested or proven, requires special sails, very expensive.

GUIDE TO SAILBOARD BOOM ASSEMBLIES

Type	Advantages	Disadvantages
Non-adjustable	Simple, lightweight, inexpensive.	Non-adaptable to a wide range of sail designs.
Adjustable with removable extensions Examples: Windsurfing Hawaii, Fleetwood	Relatively lightweight and trouble free; custom extensions offer unlimited adjustment.	Boom must have two "breaks," allowing structural and usage vulnerability. Extension pieces are easy to lose.
Telescoping adjustable booms Examples: Surfline, Pacific Sports	No extension pieces to lose track of; simple, rigid, good all-around.	Heavier than extension types, prone to jamming, prone to filling with water.

(continued)

GUIDE TO SAILBOARD BOOM ENDS (front end pieces)

Type	Advantages	Disadvantages
Popular U.S. version Example: Windsurfer type	Ties tight, has large handle, good bumper.	Doesn't tie ultra-tight.
Popular European version Example: Mistral type	Ties tight, has functional handle/bumper.	Slightly heavy, utilizes clumsy tie-on.
Popular "after-market" version Example: Windsurfing Hawaii type	Ties fairly tight, easy tie-on, strong.	No handle, can slip up and down, no bumper.
Ropeless boom ends (clamp types)	Rating pending.	Rating pending.

GUIDE TO SAILBOARD BOOM ENDS (rear pieces)

Type	Advantages	Disadvantages
Built-in pulley-type	Easy outhaul adjustment, even for hard-to-pull high performance sails.	Some brands difficult to thread (with rigging line in beach situation). Some pulleys mounted insecurely. Vulnerable to sand and grit.
Non-pulley type	Simple, adequate for most recreational use.	Limited purchase for high performance outhaul adjustment.

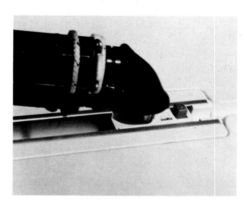

GUIDE TO MAST FOOT ATTACHMENTS

Type	Advantages	Disadvantages
Friction fit Examples: Windsurfer "T" system, expanable O-ring systems	Simple and inexpensive, detachable under load. T-systems not affected by sand and grit.	Unreliable rig attachment; liable to pop out under stress, causing injury and/or separation from board. Expandable O-ring type systems adversely affected by sand and grit.
Quick release systems (spring clip and related designs) Examples: Mistral, F-2, new Windsurfer (as of 1984)	Generally simple and reliable; some brands can be adjusted to release under pre-set loads.	Some of these designs difficult to operate and/or unreliable when contacted with sand or other foreign matter.
Semi-permanent systems Examples: Original Windsurfing Hawaii bolt-on mast base plate, triangular or star shaped screw-down plates	Very reliable in surf or high wind conditions.	Awkward to transport board with mast base attached. Sail can only be rigged when mast is attached to board.

GUIDE TO SAILBOARD MAST BASES

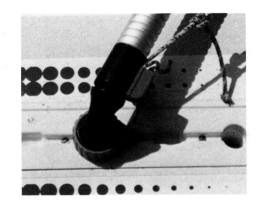

Type	Advantages	Disadvantages
Short plastic cup type; commonly 47-55mm diameter Example: Bic, Sailboard	Simple and inexpensive.	Minimal provision for downhaul adjustment and uphaul attachment. Provides no extension for high performance use. Some types have minimum extension up into the mast, risking split mast at the base.
Tall molded plastic type Example: Windsurfer	Provides moderate mast extension.	Offers only limited facility for sail adjustment. Many versions not strong enough for surf use.
Aluminum tube with cleat Example: Windsurfing Hawaii, Pacific Sports, Fleetwood, S.R.O.	Strong and reliable, most brands have good provision for downhaul adjustment, often adaptable to variety of universal systems and mast feet.	Somewhat expensive. Those with smaller diameters make for a sloppy fit in some of the larger diameter masts.
Tall, extendable aluminum base (built-in mast extension) Example: Windsurfing Hawaii, Pacific Sports	Convenient, fairly strong, good interchangability and adaptability.	Not as strong as the non-extendable type. Clumsy, especially if mounted permanently on the board. Some variations of this style use adjustment systems which are easily impaired by sand.

GUIDE TO SAILBOARD "UNIVERSAL" SYSTEMS

Type	Advantages	Disadvantages
Mechanical Example: Windsurfer	Very reliable and long lasting (although can break in the surf).	Relatively expensive, can pinch user, hard material unforgiving when bumped by user during sailing, etc., heavy.
Flexible rubber/plastic "hour glass" or tendon Example: Boge joint, Windsurfing Hawaii joint, Steamline Design tendon type	Often inexpensive, usually soft, better brands quite reliable.	Reliability varied; most should be replaced regularly.
Rope Universal Example: Bombora, California Wind Design	Inexpensive, easy to inspect for wear, lightweight.	Many types do not allow fine tuning of the downhaul. Some brands can allow the mast butt to contact the board deck, causing dents. Rigorous use speeds rope wear.

5 RIG IT RIGHT

*I*n boardsailing, rigging is a quiet and personal task. It is that fundamental preparation ritual which each skipper accomplishes a little differently from the next, adding touches of procedure and style according to individual preference. While it takes a little time, rigging prepares you for the boardsailing experience. Like a skier sharpening skis before hitting the snow or a motorcyclist tuning and fueling the machinery before surging into motion, the process of rigging saturates you with the "feel" and total mood of your endeavor. It is a brief and thoughtful exercise.

UNRAVELING THE COMPLEXITIES

The process begins with the understanding of some terms and skills. If you don't know them, you must learn them. This isn't difficult. We'll begin this chapter with a quick run-through of specific term definitions and some diagrams of knots necessary to efficient sailboard rigging. This will eliminate references to "that rope up by the front of the sail" and other confusing descriptions. There's a name and reason for every piece of equipment, every knot and every procedure. The logic of the separate parts makes for a clear overall picture. It takes minutes to become familiar with the basics, and the time spent will pay for itself in simplified set-up and take-down steps.

MAINSAIL REVIEW

Rigging a sailboard begins with the sail. As diagrammed in chapter 3, the *downhaul rope* pulls down on the bottom of sail. The *uphaul rope* pulls the sail out of the water when sailing is to begin. The *outhaul* rope pulls the "clew" of the sail out to the end of the booms. Similarly, the *leash* is the rope which "loose ties" the rig (mast and sail) to the board. The *head* of the sail is, of course, the uppermost portion of the sail. The *foot* is the entire bottom edge of the sail. Not quite as obvious are the *tack* (lower forward corner of the sail), the *clew* (aft or boom end corner of the sail), the *luff* (leading edge area of the sail), and the *leech* (trailing edge of the sail). *Battens* are stiffening strips (usually plastic) which are inserted in the sail's leech to aid sail shape.

KNOT TIPS

In order to effectively tie together, tune, and tension the sail—along with mast and booms—the board-sailor need know just a few key knots and lashings. Chief knots are the *bowline*, *figure 8* knot, and *half hitch*. Depending upon what type of equipment you have, generally you'll standardize on one or two effective lashings. The *prussic hitch*, *Windsurfing Hawaii boom lashing* and *Mistral-type "Hawaiian" boom lashings* are three excellent and commonly used examples.

These attachments are no more difficult to tie than cruder knots, but perform much better than most jury-rig set-ups. And they're much easier to adjust and untie. Follow our illustrations for some easy lessons.

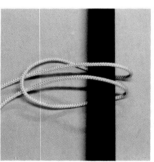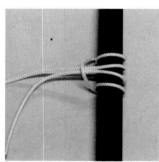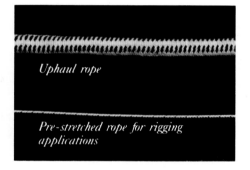

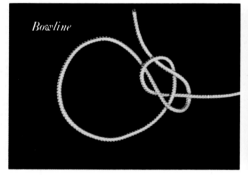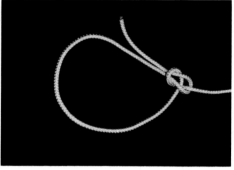

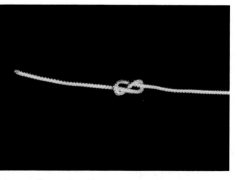

See page 61 for Windsurfing Hawaii and Mistral-type Boom Lashing

NOTES ON ROPE

Effective knots require the right rope. To begin, sailboard uphaul rope should be large diameter, hollow-core braid (preferably with a rubber bungee cord inserted in the rope's center so that the rope stays snug against the mast). Elsewhere, "yachting type" braided rope, preferably "pre-stretched" is recommended. A popular brand in this category is the British "plaited" Marlowe pre-stretched rope, recognizable by its red and black flecks in a largely white braid.

Importantly, "twisted" three strand rope, old clothes line, yellow polypropylene ski rope, sisal rope, and nylon ropes are not suitable for rigging sailboards. These do not provide the low stretch, easy handling, knot holding characteristics of braided dacron varieties.

SETTING UP THE RIG

THE RIGGING PROCEDURE

So, some assumptions. Sail, mast, and board are on the beach; clean, complete, and ship-shape. Lines (ropes) are in order, lingo is understood, and some key knots have been mastered. It's time to actually put the rig together, plug it into the board, and go sailing!

1 Pull the sail sock over the mast (being careful there are no twists) and tension the downhaul a bit so that you will not tie your booms where they can interfere with later downhaul adjustment. Insert any mid-leech battens. Now slip the mast base into the mast.

2 Then stand the mast upright, noting the height at which you will want to attach the booms. (Boom height is a matter of personal preference; if you're just beginning, don't be afraid to "guesstimate," using common sense.)

3 Lay the mast down again. Now slip the boom assembly, front end first, over and down the mast until the front boom end is at approximately the spot you've just picked out. Do not attach the booms closer than two or three inches below the top of the sock opening, or you may not be able to downhaul sufficiently later. And make sure not to pinch the luff sock in the boom jaws.

4 Next, with the booms lying parallel to the mast, front end at the sock opening and rear end toward the mast tip, tie the boom assembly to the mast. Do so just as tightly as you can. At this point you have the leverage to crack or break your mast, so proceed carefully.

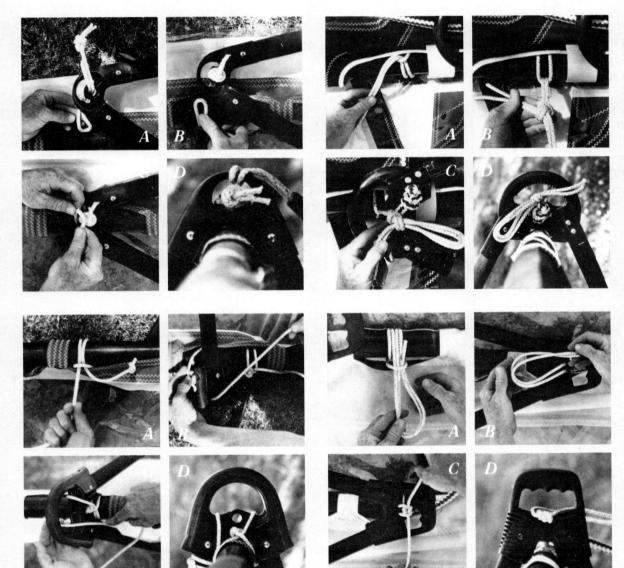

Far left: popular "after-market" Windsurfing Hawaii boom assembly is especially effective for rigs which are "water started" and do not require an uphaul.

Left: Excellent O'brien boom assembly is well designed and durable.

Far left: Common European Mistral-type boom assembly involves complex knot work but is well known and popular.

Left: Standard U.S. Windsurfer boom assembly is simple and effective, but not noted for superior durability.

5 Pull the rear (aft end) of the boom assembly down until the booms are roughly perpendicular to the mast. Do this gingerly, as excessive force applied to a too tightly lashed boom can crush the mast. So if you feel excessive resistance or hear creaking noises, stop and loosen the lashing slightly.

6 Now, pull the outhaul through the aft boom fitting, bringing the clew of the sail toward the boom end. Tension the sail firmly and cleat the outhaul.

Left to right, European Mistral-type outhaul system; popular "after-market" Windsurfing Hawaii outhaul system; common pulley system outhaul such as that found on O'brien sailboard.

7 Lastly, the downhaul. Some skippers loosely tension the downhaul before tying on the boom assembly, while others don't mess with the downhaul until booms are in place. Either attack will work. Reeve the downhaul through whatever system of leads or blocks (pulleys) is provided, and apply moderate tension.

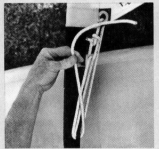

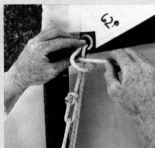

RIG REFINEMENT

Fine tuning of a sailboard sail and rig is a subject of real depth and detail. Following are some rig refinements which will get your equipment in order and get you on the water.

1 Pull the outhaul until the sail has a fairly flat look and is relatively wrinkle-free.

2 Cinch the downhaul until most of the horizontal wrinkles have disappeared (yet allowing a hint of vertical wrinkle running parallel with the mast). You'll have to use some muscle here.

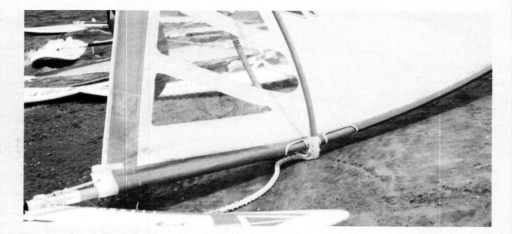

3 Once the sail is tensioned, be sure that the outhaul and downhaul are securely cleated or tied off.

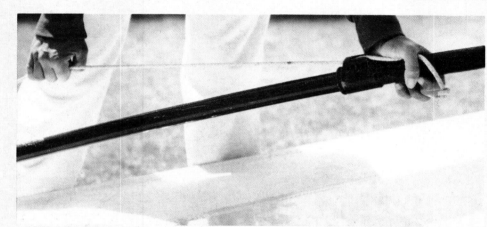

4 Finally, insert and tension any head or full battens in your sail. (Although not all boardsails need battens, most modern sail designs incorporate them). Batten ''retention'' systems vary, but most are self explanatory, utilizing batten pockets with elastic or velcro retainers.

SPOT CHECK: BOARD AND COMPONENTS

Now that the sail and rig are ready for sailing, give your board and components an inspection.

1 Be sure the skeg is securely attached. Although infrequent, "slide-in," "screw-in," and also other skeg types can occasionally loosen with use.

2 Check mast attachment fittings for firm assembly and working integrity; Make sure they are free of sand or other obstructions.

3 Inspect all rubber "hourglass" and/or "power joint" universal fittings to ensure proper working order and adjustment.

RIG-TO-BOARD

With most modern sailboard equipment, attaching the rig to the board is a quick and simple procedure. But this attachment is critical to accomplish correctly—both for successful sailing results and for safety. So for the record, any board having a rig-to-hull connection which has even the slightest chance of coming apart while in use should have a safety line (leash) connecting rig to hull. This way, in the event of capsize the rig can't blow away from the board when disattached, leaving you stranded in a body of water somewhere! Experienced sailors will agree: abide by this prudent practice.

1 Affix your rig to your board.

2 Insert the daggerboard (or lower the centerboard).

3 Place the board down in some shallow water. Time to go sailing!

PERFORMANCE RIGGING

ADVANCED RIGGING

Sailboarding is a sport of spectrums. Through the maturity of time and the creations of technology, the high performance pursuits in the sport have brought about equipment and corresponding rigging aspects that extend beyond the realm of simple recreational sailing.

You may not want to incorporate pieces of this "high performance spectrum" into your own sailing; however most avid boardsailors can't resist at least a step or two into the "twilight zone" of "max" tuning.

PRO TOUCHES

Although we've covered the material necessary for basic profi-ciency in matters of rigging concepts and procedures, there exists a separate realm of boardsailing sophistication that exceeds the normal. This is the world of special technical innovation for high performance competitors in course racing and wave riding.

While impossible to cover the vast spectrum of boardsailing's "pro touches" within this short chapter, the essential components can be shown in short order. So let's take a look at some of the hardware and tuning techniques that aid the experts in sailing so efficiently and so fast. You may decide not to incorporate any of these bits, pieces, and ideas into your own sailing program, but most boardsailors seem to end up employing at least some of the

technology which "was the latest thing in Hawaii just last week." Following is a selection of items that have found appeal and acceptance.

THE HARNESS

The harness enables a boardsailor to lean back and relax while at planing speed. This conserves energy and increases the sailor's ability to extract maximum performance from both board and rig.

Rigging harness lines on your booms is a simple, inexpensive procedure—probably one you'll want to try out. Harness set-ups come in a wide variety of styles, from velcro-closure preassembled models to simple "tie the rope to the boom" types. (Most booms now come with soft, comfortable grips which can be damaged by harness lines which tie directly onto the boom grip area). The velcro-type harness fittings just wrap around the boom arm and stick together. A third, and very common harness line attachment is via pads or "grips" through which the line is reeved (see illustration). This has proven popular and quite workable. An effective refinement in harness line set-up is the bungee cord "retainer" which keeps the harness rope taut against the boom yet offers a convenient loop to hook your harness buckle into.

Harness line set-up reduces sailor's fatigue, and increases efficiency. Harness should fit snugly; "hooking up" requires one quick motion.

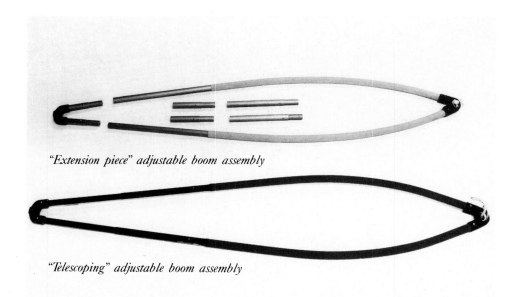

"Extension piece" adjustable boom assembly

"Telescoping" adjustable boom assembly

ADJUSTABLE BOOMS

Evolution of sail design has prompted a number of rigging improvements. Adjustable booms are perhaps the best known of these advances. There are two basic styles: 1) those which adjust by means of a telescoping function, 2) and those which adjust by means of removable extension pieces. The advent of adjustable booms has made it possible for sailors at all levels of ability to enjoy the advantages offered by shorter boomed sails in higher winds. For more information on booms, see chapter 4, Sails, Masts, & Components.

HI-TECH OUTHAUL AND DOWNHAUL

Another more recent advance in rigging technology which has come as a result of sail development is the application of block and tackle (pulley) systems to outhaul and downhaul tuning. These systems, which often provide purchase power of 4:1 or 5:1, have become popular as sail designs necessitated increased rig tension for proper adjustment. While they're not absolutely necessary on many recrea-

tional rigs, block and tackle set-ups afford easy and precise adjustment for sailors of varying physical strength capacities. A good pulley system reduces the sheer muscle needed to get your rig tuned and tight. But a word of caution here: sails not designed for use with pulley systems will probably not be fitted with tack or clew rings sufficient to withstand the increased stress load. Watch your sail for signs of damage to the tack and clew rings if you begin using a pulley/hook system. Damage spotted before total ring failure can usually be inexpensively and quickly repaired by any competent sailmaker.

TELLTALES & STREAMERS

Telltales are nothing new. But many amateur sailors neglect them. Experts don't. It's common to see four to eight foot length nylon or dacron "streamers" flying from the mastheads of sailboards during a race. While great for looks, these streamers can be helpful in pointing out the "apparent" wind direction, especially on points of sail near to dead downwind. Similarly, telltales (very small streamers made from spinnaker cloth, recording tape, yarn, etc.) attached to the leech of the sail can help you determine correct sail trim. Telltales, when floating freely in the breeze, are

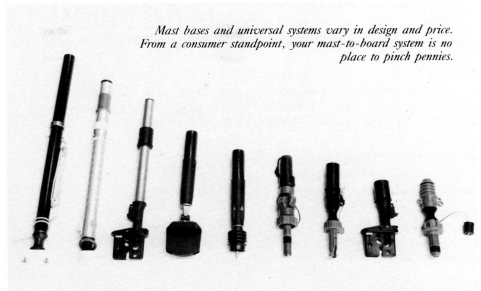

Mast bases and universal systems vary in design and price. From a consumer standpoint, your mast-to-board system is no place to pinch pennies.

helpful performance antennae that'll help you beat your buddy across the bay!

MAST EXTENSIONS AND BASES

Increased variety in sail design is also responsible for the growing popularity of mast extensions and adjustable mast bases (see chapter 4). Masts can be made taller to accommodate newer, higher aspect ratio sail designs. This can be done by: 1) adding a tubular aluminum extension between the mast and mast base, 2) by utilizing an adjustable mast base, 3) or via the use of a short extention piece plugged into the top of the mast. Extreme care must be taken not to over extend the mast, as this can lead to mast breakage (most often at the very bottom of the spar or at the revised point of boom attachment). Most reputable sailboard dealers can reinforce masts against such potential problems for a reasonable fee.

MAST TRACKS

Sliding mast tracks (those that can be adjusted while sailing) are a fairly recent development which has been especially useful on World Cup race boards. These tracks allow the mast to be slid forward for maximum waterline length and upwind ability for race course weather legs—in addition to aft adjustment for efficient body and rig position, plus wetted surface reduction for windy reaching legs.

For recreational sailing, sliding mast tracks often go unused and just get in the way. But competition minded funboard sailors can profit from them if proper skill is applied.

FOOTSTRAPS

Attached to the board in strategic location for weight position and balance, footstraps keep you secure on the board in high speed bouncy conditions, providing stability, control, and leverage for advanced "foot steering" maneuvers. Developed during the early years of performance boardsailing breakthroughs, footstraps continue to grow in popularity and are utilized effectively on World Cup boards, wave boards, funboards, and an array of other racing, recreational, and specialty boards. Available in various brands and materials, good foostraps should be durable, adjustable, and well-padded.

BOOM GRIPS

Boom grip materials have been

the focus of considerable research and development. Ideally, boom grips should be easy on the hands but also durable and wear resistant. Although the time tested conventional rubber grip is as acceptable as ever, newer foam grips offer lighter weight, increased traction, and more comfort. But they do give away some durability to the more common rubber grips.

BOARD CHECK

Although this is a chapter on rigging and set-up, no rig is any good without a decently assembled board! Many sailors spend lots of time and money on sophisticated rigging procedures and equipment while neglecting simple attention to board basics. So, while these matters are covered more fully in chapters 5 and 10, let this serve as a primer: 1) a clean board will move through the water better than a dirty, sticky board, 2) skeg and daggerboard efficiency can be maximized by secure attachment, careful alignment, and clean foils (file the chips and scratches for smoothness), 3) skeg and daggerboard choice is personal and affects performance; sometimes the "stock" items are best and sometimes "after market" accessories are better. This is a matter of research and experimentation.

DE-RIGGING

Strange sort of word? Not really. What you rig, you must de-rig! Let's presume that we've had a pleasant and uneventful day of sailing and we're back at the beach. (No broken stuff, untied knots, lost battens, etc. means that all rigging was right and proper indeed). De-rigging is, of course, just a reversal of the rigging process. However there are a few tricks worth mentioning and a few practices which if followed will prevent lots of frustration.

UNKNOTTING KNOTS

If you find you have inadvertently tied the wrong type of knot, so much for efficiency. Marshal your patience and get out the pocket knife. All in all, it's far and away best to tie the right knots in the first place.

COPING WITH COMPONENTS

Take apart, fresh water wash, and preferably leave apart components such as boom and mast extensions that fit to close tolerances. Do this periodically, if not after every sail, so that set-up next time is from scratch for the specific conditions on hand. It's awful to arrive at the beach on the best day of the year only to find that you're unable to adjust your mast or booms to your small high wind sails. Now is also a good time to inspect all vulnerable (mechanical or wear prone) parts. You'll be much happier shopping for a new hour-glass universal after work or on your lunch break rather than when the wind's blowing next weekend.

SAIL HABITS

It probably won't be possible to get your sail perfectly clean and dry before you leave the sailing site, but try to keep it as clean as you can, and store it carefully until the next use. Sail storage techniques vary, but acceptable methods range from, 1) taking the sail off the mast and rolling it from the head to the foot, 2) to rolling the sail from the clew to the mast and slipping it all into a rig bag with booms left attached or, 3) removing the booms and wrapping the sail around the mast. Method number one is the best, though others are satisfactory.

FINAL TOUCHES

Finally, when you've finished de-rigging, check the immediate area before you leave to be sure you aren't forgetting any of your

gear. Items most frequently left on the beach include battens, daggerboards, wetsuits (especially booties), towels, and harnesses. A quick look around is an inexpensive insurance policy!

If you're the kind of person who really likes to take extra good care of your equipment, a little time spent on maintenance after you get home is advisable. Rinse your sail with freshwater, get everything dry, inspect once more for unnoticed damage, and put all equipment and parts carefully away in a place that's safe from automobile grease droppings, paint, sharp objects, and other natural enemies.

Armed with a solid understanding of rigging procedures and basic concepts, there's only one thing left to do: look forward to the next day of sailing and the trouble-free fun you'll have!

6 BASIC SKILLS & EQUIPMENT

"Just a single one hour lesson—free with your new board—will getcha on your way"..."Just eighteen hours of easy lessons—at only $49.95 an hour and you'll be boardsailing with the best of 'em!"..."Lessons? No need for lessons; why this board is so smart it'll sail itself but we'll throw in this here how-they-do-it manual at no extra charge and you'll be scootin' around the water mighty fast!"

Like all skills, boardsailing must be learned, and some ways of learning are more effective than others. All of the examples above would be, let's say, less than ideal learning programs—*far less than ideal*. But most experts agree on a few things: 1) good lessons afford fast, relatively trouble-free learning, 2) good beginner's equipment speeds up learning, 3) the first few hours of lessons, trial, and error are the most difficult in the learning process. Like learning to ride a bicycle, everything comes much easier once you're familiar with the sensation and achieve a sense of balance.

TO BEGIN

It is entirely possible to learn boardsailing by yourself through trial and error. But few would advise it. Lessons are available from almost all reputable sailboard dealers in

addition to programs offered through city parks and recreation departments and other selected organizations. Normally, lessons are not expensive and besides, they're fun. Sailboard manufacturers are enthusiastic promoters of good lesson programs, and often their dealers include them with a board purchase. So, there are very few reasons not to take lessons. They're beneficial in more ways than one and are highly recommendable.

THE LESSON METHOD

A good lesson program, administered by a good instructor, answers questions automatically and solves problems quickly. You learn with consultation and guidance, minimizing frustration and eliminating the bewilderment that sometimes accompanies a new challenge.

Initial learning takes place on a land simulator—a modified board and rig device which simulates boardsailing sensations in a controlled (and dry) setting. Instructors explain wind direction, wind strength, direction of movement, weight distribution, water safety and, of course, all about the board and sail. Equipment, usually provided, consists of "trainer" boards and sails which aid the sailboard beginner. Foot movement, hand position, posture, and other essential matters of technique are demonstrated and students are coached through the skills. The experience is both social and individual, providing personal challenge and shared fun.

THE DIE HARD METHOD

As mentioned, you *can* learn to boardsail by yourself—but it's awkward—and sometimes downright tough. Following is an excerpt from a gentleman describing his first time boardsailing while on a tropical vacation:

I joyfully declined any instructions from the young man who rented me the board. I assured him I was a born snow skier and could learn boardsailing best by myself.

Maneuvering my board out from the beach to deeper waters, it occurred to me that the water temperature was so very pleasant at this tropical latitude. ...In due course I was to find out exactly how fortunate that was...

I lifted myself jauntily onto the board, the sail floating in the water. Before I could even stand up straight I re-entered the water with involuntary urgency. ...Okay then. So the young joker back there on the beach had given me a funny-board.

With dogged determination I struggled back on the board, only to taste the salty tang of sea water seconds later. When I had finally found my balance, I was facing what proved to be a formidable task: that of pulling up the sail. During the next fifteen minutes I performed some dazzling acrobatic dives. And the water seemed to hold some special attraction for me, for I was returning to it with frequency.

The young board concessionaire on the beach was by now joined by other spectators, obviously all fascinated by my show. My first successful effort in raising the sail produced a loud cheer and a full round of applause. But the accolade was short-lived, or so it seemed, because it's difficult to hear when you're underwater.

Spurred on by such "motivating" interest from the crowd, I mustered all my strength and balance, ignoring the chafes and bruises from gymnastics with board, booms, and mast. But it was either me or "it" now, and I would conquer the odds at all costs!

Finally I succeeded in getting the sail up and into the wind, sailing away from the beach with increasing speed. The sweet surge of success swelled within me as I pitter-pattered over the water's surface. My excursion, however, was short. Even in the sparse breeze of the afternoon I managed the

impossible—a radical wipeout. Sail went over, I went down, board went thataway....

Back on the beach I was regarded as a major entertainment star. Humiliated and fatigued, I accepted the help of my seven-year-old son in getting board and rig back to the shore. Later that afternoon my wife decided to give boardsailing a fateful try. After some slight splashing and balancing, she got the hang of it and sailed back and forth along the beach for a full forty-five minutes. So who needs sailboard lessons anyway? My wife sure didn't....

FREE AND EASY

Although the simplicity of sailboarding is a marvelous thing, considerations as to clothing, equipment, and weather protection can make a differnce as to the quality of the whole experience. As in all sports, what you wear, what you use, and how you're prepared all directly affect the results of a day of "doing your thing." Weather conditions, sailing gear, tools and spares, safe transport, provisions for food and drink; these are as much a part of a day of sailing as planing along in a stiff breeze.

Everyone has their own procedure for getting ready to go boardsailing. It's a matter of style. Remember that you will be exposed to wind, sun, wetness, other boards and boats—and a myriad of people and situations. Safety and comfort play a big part in preserving good times in the face of all the activity and energy that sailboarding involves.

WHAT TO WEAR

If it's warm, you don't have to wear much...that's the luxury of it. Guys wear trunks and girls wear bikinis or one-piece suits—very little else. But safety and convenience, in addition to common public boating laws dictate bringing along a few extra provisions.

LIFE VESTS AND HARNESSES

At this writing, 37 U.S. states require the use of Coast Guard approved life vests on sailboards. Available in various styles, these "approved" vests have developed the reputation of sometimes being prohibitively bulky. However, some modern designs are quite streamlined. Visit your dealer for a look at the various styles.

Harnesses, also available in myriad types and price ranges, are excellent for the purpose of "hooking up"

WEATHER PROTECTION

U.S. Coast Guard approved harness/life vest

to the boom and reducing tension on the arms from holding on. But to date, few harnesses meet Coast Guard safety vest requirements. If your state requires approved vests, an ideal solution is a harness (like the one pictured here) that doubles as an approved safety vest. Your dealer should be able to assist here.

HAND PROTECTION

Holding onto a sailboard boom during long periods of sailing can be hard on the hands. As a result, some sailors use gloves for protection, especially in cold weather. The hands of World Cup racers and Hawaiian surfsailors are a sight to behold; large, hard callouses on fingers and palms that would make a jack hammer operator feel like a sissy in comparison. But not everyone wants those callouses—and good sailing gloves are helpful here.

Most sailboard dealers carry a selection of gloves, both full fingered and half fingered. Some are leather, while others are of flexible synthetic materials. Choice is a very personal consideration. Most experienced sailors insist that it's important to retain a good "feel," thus an excessively bulky or stiff glove would be undesirable. Don't hesitate to be picky in your choice.

BOOTIES

Like sailing gloves, booties aid grip and also offer protection. But since the feet are more naturally callused than the hands, the larger benefit of booties is that they keep your feet warm in cold weather. Some types have thick, almost topsider-like soles, whereas others are made of thin wetsuit neoprene and offer footing that's almost like being bare-

foot. Naturally the latter have a short life, whereas the thicker varieties last longer but enable less "feel" on the board surface.

HOT WEATHER

When the sun is bright and you intend to go out for a long day of sailing, take care not to get roasted. On those really "perfect" days it's surprisingly easy to get wrapped up in the beauty of all the elements—sparkling water, beautiful sails, smooth sailing, hot sun. But watch out for those ultraviolet rays. They can have unrelenting after effects.

EYE WEAR

Sun glasses are an important asset, especially in mid-day when glare is severe. Some sailors prefer the new, goggle-like unbreakables, while others use expensive glass-lens wire or plastic rim sun glasses. These are best secured with a safety strap around the back of the neck. Polarized lenses are highly desirable;

they are particularly effective in reducing glare caused from the sun's reflection on the water.

CLOTHING AND SUN PROTECTION

For persons who tend to sunburn easily, a lightweight long sleeved shirt, jersey, or windbreaker and a good sun visor are essentials. Besides being practical, these kinds of clothing are available in great styles and colors. Protective skin lotions provide supplementary covering and can be kept handy in a carry bag or harness pocket for repeated applications as needed. Although modern science has produced many new superior "sun block" lotions, traditional Zinc Oxide ointment is still widely used for the nose and lower lip, both of which are exposed to the sun at all times.

The deception involved in warm weather sailing is that you are continually being cooled with wet spray. It's a delicious combination, but the cool water doesn't reduce the intensity of the sun. Be aware of the elements and take necessary precautions.

COLD WEATHER PROTECTION

Cold weather sailing on a sailboard can be a crisp and invigorating experience, but what you wear can make or break your physical endurance, your state of mind, and your sailing. A wetsuit or drysuit ensures warmth, thus aids comfort, endurance, and physical strength.

WETSUIT

A wetsuit has several advantages. It is lightweight, flexible, and fits snugly to your body, allowing easy movement. It is warm, and as water seeps into the suit your body temperature heats it immediately and maintains body temperature or

better. Wetsuit configurations offer versatility; among them the full-leg, long sleeved ''farmer John,'' the armless full-leg ''farmer John,'' and half-suits or ''vests'' in many varieties. Wetsuit thicknesses are wide ranging, the thickest providing the best warmth and the thinnest offering the best freedom of movement. Modern suits, such as the excellent examples pictured here, come in attractive designs and semifitted sizes.

DRYSUIT

Here is an interesting asset to the boardsailor. While popular in Europe and also widely accepted for other kinds of water applications, the drysuit has been somewhat ignored by U.S. boardsailors. Clearly, price has been a factor in this. A drysuit generally costs 10% to 30% more than a quality full coverage wetsuit.

But development in drysuit design has been significant, and boardsailors can benefit from this. Like a wetsuit, a drysuit is essentially a rubber body suit designed for warmth and freedom of movement. Unlike a wetsuit, however, a drysuit is ''sealed'' at the neck, wrists, and

ankles, admitting no water. Some drysuits even have soft pile inner lining for comfort.

In practical use, most drysuit users report at least some kind of water leakage, but benefits over wetsuits are impressive. With a drysuit there is no initial ''cold water shock'' when entering the water for the first time. A drysuit has a much lighter effective weight than a wetsuit because it is not water filled. Water is heavy. The slight accumulation of air in a drysuit provides extra buoyancy for the sailor in case of a fall in the water, thus making it easier to get back up on the board and get going. Drysuits can be both warmer than wetsuits and cooler. Warm clothing can be worn under a drysuit, or just a bathing suit, as necessary. Perspiration rate is somewhat controllable; beneficial because excessive perspiration depletes the body of salt, risking cramping and fatigue.

Although usually very durable, drysuits are not completely indestructable. A cut or torn drysuit in very cold conditions could cause severe ''cold shock'' and possibly life threatening hypothermia. And a water filled drysuit could conceiv-

ably be dangerously heavy. But track record in boardsailing, scuba diving, and other applications reflects substantial overall safety.

''AFTER-SAIL'' CLOTHING

What a joy to slip into something dry and comfortable after boardsailing! An ideal answer for this in most situations is a warm-up suit or pile jacket with sweat pants or the like. In hot weather, often a long or short sleeved T-Shirt and bermuda shorts will do the trick. It's a good idea to have beach towels handy (bring an extra for the friend who forgot), and in cold weather it's highly recommendable to have a wool blanket or two on hand.

Footwear (sandals, tennies, etc.) is useful for warmth and also for protecting feet on rocky beaches or parking lots where broken glass, tin cans, and splintered wood might be strewn about. For those who desire a freshwater shower, inexpensive solar heated portable ''sun showers'' are available and becoming popular. These can be found at most general marine stores.

BOARDSAILING GEAR

Despite the fact that much of sailboarding's appeal has been based on its simplicity and freedom from "hassles," it's pretty common for sailors (at one time or another) to experience the frustration of arriving at some remote sailing site with lunch all packed, sail, rig, and board carefully tied atop the car, and the daggerboard at home in the garage. A checklist of gear and a bag of tools and spares can turn a minor mess into a helpful little miracle.

Following is a list of items that can make a boardsailor's journey to the beach worry-free from sunrise to sunset:

Spare Rope—carry at least two different varieties, sufficient to replace an uphaul, outhaul, downhaul, or assist in a safety emergency.

Tools—a mini-kit should include pliers, screwdrivers, appropriate allen wrenches, pocket knife, rigging knife, hack saw, crescent wrench and socket set to replace a power joint or universal if necessary.

Duct Tape—the super stick, super durable, all weather temporary fixer (works much better than bubble gum or hot tempered foot stomping).

Spare sail battens—at least one full set and preferably two.

Additional sails—not absolutely necessary but recommendable; one or two back-up sails of different sizes are useful in setting up your rig for specific variances in wind and weather.

Spare harness (or at least harness hook)—for harness users who experience harness seam, strap, or hook failure.

Safety Equipment—especially important for sailing any real distance from shore: flares, strobe lights, die markers, flotation vests.

While the above items may seem to add up to one heck of a lot of gear, they can actually be stowed in one large or two medium sized duffle bags. And the bags will fit easily in your car trunk or back seat. There's no substitute for being well set-up and prepared.

MASTERING THE BASICS

Okay. Once again some assumptions. You've gone through the paces with board and rig and understand how it's all put together. You can rig and de-rig your equipment, and with gear in hand you're ready to pick a spot and get to boardsailing!

WHERE TO LEARN

If you're taking lessons, the boardsailing school instructor will of course determine the sailing location. But no matter who determines the particular site, it's important. Experts agree that as a beginner you should begin boardsailing at a place that: 1) has a steady light wind, 2) has a beach which allows

a gradual water entry and doesn't get too deep too soon, 3) is away from powerboats, fishing lines, and other water traffic, 4) and is close to shore.

Whether you are learning from a certified instructor, by yourself, or being coached by a friend, a calm and controlled setting will ensure the quickest progress and highest degree of safety. Ideal winds are from 5 to 7-knots and the water surface should be ripply-smooth. Avoid choppy water, any substantial currents, and be cautious of ocean shore or large lake situations in which the wind is blowing toward open ocean. You don't want to be blown out to sea!

SAFETY SUGGESTIONS

If it's even slightly cold, don't risk overexposure. Wear a wetsuit, drysuit, and/or life vest according to your needs as described in this chapter. Some school instructors advise wearing booties or deck shoes on your feet. This is a good idea because board decks have non-slip rough surfaces and beach areas often have rocks, shells, sticks, broken glass, and other obstacles which can cause damage to your feet. Use your best judgement here, depending upon the sailing site and conditions.

When out in the water, don't get separated from your board. Naturally, learning will involve falling in the water many times. Treat your board as your island. It's a safety base for flotation and relative dryness. Make sure your rig and board stay together, as the sail forms a surface anchor when lying in the water. This helps retard drift and increases your visibility. If rig and board separate for any reason, do your best to re-adjoin them but the first priority doesn't change; stay with the board and function from there.

PREPARE TO LAUNCH

This is the easy part. Just carry your board and sail to the water. There is a little bit of technique necessary to do this; your sail is best carried above your head with the booms aligned parallel to the wind direction. This way the sail won't fill with air and become uncontrollable. Your board is carried (some folks partially drag it) with deck toward the body and daggerboard raised or removed until just before the board is ready to go in the water. Different sailors employ different procedures in preparing to launch. Basically you want to get to the shore without any snags or awkwardness and then finish up rig-to-board and daggerboard details just before you launch.

DIRECTION

Which way is the wind blowing and which way are you going? Needless to say, these are legitimate considerations! It's easiest to learn boardsailing with your back to the wind. So, once the wind direction is determined you can situate board and rig in the water to your best advantage. Wind direction can be identified by looking at a nearby flag or wind-sock. If no such thing is in sight, use your sail telltales or simply throw grass or

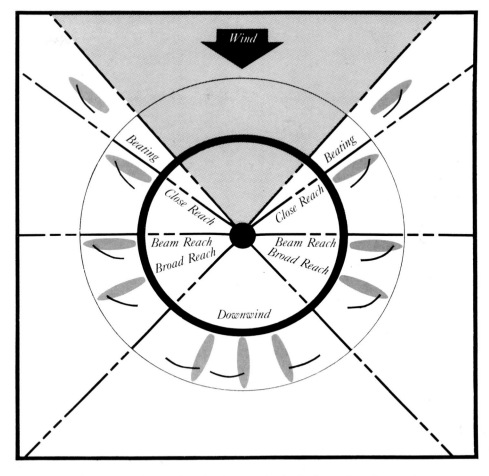

leaves in the air and watch which way they go.

Take a good look at the water around you and make sure that once under way there will be no obstacles in your path.

There are three general angles in which any sailboat (sailboards included) can be directed to generate forward movement: 1) toward the wind ("to weather"), 2) Away from the wind ("downwind"), 3) Abeam of the wind ("reaching"). The skill of sailing requires handling the board effectively on each of these different "points of sail."

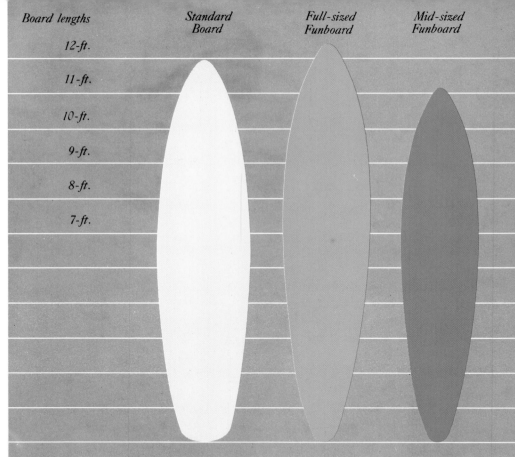

Board lengths	Standard Board	Full-sized Funboard	Mid-sized Funboard
12-ft.			
11-ft.			
10-ft.			
9-ft.			
8-ft.			
7-ft.			

Top Left: Sailboarder's drysuit offers versatility and is increasing in popularity.
Above: Standard fins and daggerboards vary in size and configuration. Stability is the objective; make your choice not by looks, but by recommendation and hands-on testing.
Right: Modern wetsuits are available in myriad styles, cuts, and thicknesses. There is literally a wetsuit for everyone.
Top (middle): Today's boards vary not only in size but in type and purpose. Standard "long board" is the most versatile, however funboards and wave boards offer exhilarating specialized performance.

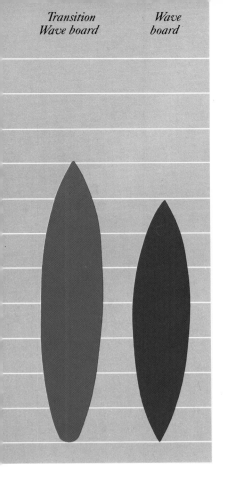

Transition
Wave board

Wave
board

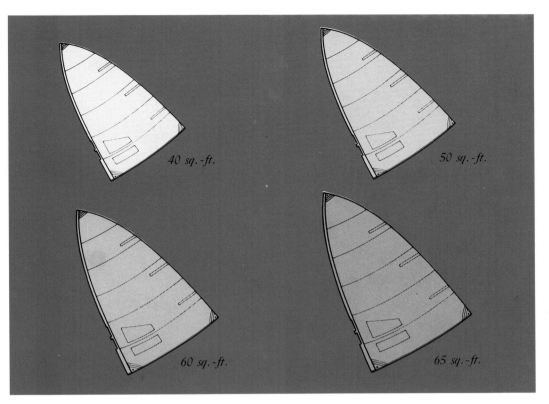

40 sq.-ft.

50 sq.-ft.

60 sq.-ft.

65 sq.-ft.

Top: Standard sails are crafted in many sizes, accommodating wind conditions, board size, and sailor's weight. Common beginner's sail encompasses 40-square feet of "sail area," whereas average recreational sail encompasses 60 to 70-square feet.

Above Right: Boardsailor's harnesses come in many shapes, colors, and prices. Quality construction and personal fit are of prime importance.

Bottom: Sweats, T-shirts and towels are ideal for after-sail comfort.

BASIC SKILLS

CLIMB ABOARD

There comes a time when the fruits of planning and discussion must be enjoyed. Climb onto your sailboard and get set to go. Put one knee aboard and hoist yourself into a standing position, keeping knees slightly sprung for good balance. At this stage, just get the feel of how the board rocks side-to-side in the water.

Clearly an established learning device is the undersized sail. With this, you can master the fundamentals of boardsailing and not be blown off balance by a large sail that harnesses a lot of wind. It's like learning to drive a car that has a small engine; if you accidentally stomp on the gas peddle you'll just speed up a little instead of lurching wildly forward.

1 Seemingly awkward at first, a sailboard sail must be lifted into an upright position from the water where it lies when the board is stationary. Make sure that your back is to the wind, the board is perpendicular to the wind, and the tip of the mast is pointing directly away from the wind.

2 With knees bent, back kept straight, and feet centered crossways on the board (one on each side of the mast base), bend down and take hold of the uphaul. Pulling the uphaul hand over hand, slowly hoist the sail into an upright position. It will become lighter while raised, as water drains off.

3 When the sail is fully raised, grip the uphaul at or nearest the boom handle and allow the sail to direction itself freely, like a wind vane. At this point you may still feel awkward, but stay loose and keep that back straight. Things will begin to come together.

HANDS AND ARMS

Beginning boardsailors often battle to control the sail with their hands and arm muscles. While some strength and a good grip are assets, sail control comes from a combination of balance and weight leverage. Proper coordination of hands and arms is more important than sheer muscle power.

1 With sail raised and your balance achieved, it's time to take hold of the boom. This will enable you to control the sail and get going. Grip the boom with both hands, one in back of the boom handle and the other 2-3 feet back from the handle. Your hands should be positioned roughly shoulder length apart on the boom. Transfer of your hands from the uphaul to the boom may at first seem tricky but

it's really quite systematic. Keeping hold of the uphaul with the arm and hand that face the board's stern, cross your other arm over and get a grip on the boom near the mast. Then release the uphaul and with your free hand grip the boom 2-3 feet back from the mast.

2 Your *mast hand* (the hand nearest the mast), controls vertical mast angle. This will determine your direction. Your other hand, *the sheet hand*, is used for "sheeting in and out," or controlling the sail's angle to the wind. This determines how much wind is harnessed and thus how much power you will capture with the sail.

3 To sheet in, pull the sail toward you with your sheet hand. Generally some arm muscle will be needed here, but there's no need to upset your balance and nothing is gained by tensing up. If wind pressure on the sail is too great, just use your sheet hand to sheet out and release the power in the sail gently, while bringing your body weight back to the board's centerline.

4 Guide the sail with your arms, while holding onto the boom with a firm (not too tight) grip. By keeping your back straight, body loose, and leaning back, your body will counterbalance the wind force on the sail.

DIRECTION OF MOVEMENT

By now you'll be moving forward and, strangely enough, once under way things get easier. But some technique is necessary to control your direction.

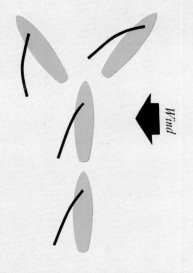

1 To head up (sail closer to the direction from which the wind is coming), angle or "rake" the mast aft—toward the rear of the board. This motion moves the board's "center of effort" aft, thus pushing the stern of the board away from the wind and the bow of the board toward the wind with the stationary daggerboard or centerboard becoming the pivot point (center of lateral resistance).

2 To bear off, or steer away from the wind direction, rake the mast forward. This moves the "center of effort" forward, forcing the board's stern toward the wind and thus moving the bow away from the wind.

3 To sail an essentially straight line, position the mast in a vertical position with no appreciable forward or aft rake.

STANCE AND TRIM

Needless to say, your board works best in the water when it's balanced properly from nose to tail (bow to stern) and side-to-side. When your board is moving at best efficiency over the water's surface it is "in trim." This is achieved by good stance, good sailing posture, and good sail control. Each of these elements assists the other.

1 With your back straight and knees bent, the arm of your mast hand should be bent at the elbow and flexible, your sheet hand extended rearward for sail control as earlier described.

2 Your feet should be crossways on the board, centered side-to-side, one on each side of the mast base, front and rear.

3 As wind fills the sail, *lean back* for balance, not forward. If the sail pulls you to leeward (away from the wind and toward a belly flop in the water), just sheet out as described above; let the sail out with your aft hand, allowing mast, boom, and sail to pivot with your mast hand and wrist.

4 If you completely lose control of the sail and begin to get off balance, quickly revert to your grip on the uphaul nearest the mast handle. You can re-group from here.

5 With increased wind strength and some sailing practice under your belt, you can modify foot position by standing with both feet behind the mast base, mast hand arm outstretched, and the mast angled toward your body or "to windward."

FALLING IN THE WATER

All boardsailors fall in the water. Some laugh at it, some scowl at it, some do it more than others. Getting back on your board and back into gear after a fall becomes pretty automatic, but the following steps will help ease the procedure.

1 In that split second when you know you're going to fall and can't reverse the inevitable, let go of the rig and try to fall to windward while the sail falls to leeward. It's best not to fall into the sail. If falling into the sail is unavoidable, at least soften the impact as best you can and stay clear of mast and boom. If you fall backwards (to windward) with the sail on top of you, reach an arm up so as to distance yourself from the sail and boom. Once in the water, feel your way along the sail and out from under. If there is trapped air under the sail you can find your way out by sight rather than just by feel.

2 Don't waste energy trying to swim the mast back into a leeward direction. Take your time, conserve energy, and get back on the board comfortably.

3 Once back in a standing position with uphaul in hand, repeat the sail raising procedure as earlier shown. If you find your back is not to the wind and the mast is not pointing to leeward, raise the sail up to about 30 degrees above the water and hold it in that position. Like a weather vane, the sail will utilize the wind and gradually work its way to leeward. As the sail does this, you can leverage yourself against its stability-force and rotate the board back into its perpendicular-to-the-wind position with your feet. Strange as it may seem, this works in practice much more easily than it is explained.

POINTS OF SAIL

As earlier described, a sailing craft (sailboards included) can essentially move in three directional modes; toward the wind, away from the wind, and abeam, or side-or-wind. No craft can sail directly into the eye of the wind.

At any given time you're sailing on "a tack." When you are sailing along with your left hand closest to the mast you are on a *port tack*. When your right hand is closest to the mast you are on a *starboard tack*. By pivoting the bow of the board across the eye of the wind you can "change tacks," thus altering your course direction.

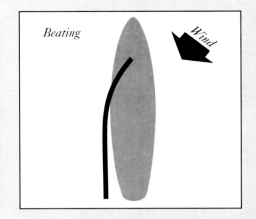

Beating

1 *Sailing to weather* or "beating" is sailing toward the wind as close to its point of origin as possible. A well tuned, well-skippered sailboard can achieve an angle of 45-degrees "off the wind." Pointing the board any closer than this toward the wind will result in efficiency loss and retarded forward movement. To sail to weather successfully, stay "close hauled" with sail sheeted in (close to your body) and mast ver-

tical or angled slightly windward. The primary goal is to keep the board moving as fast and as "high" into the wind as possible, in "the groove." If you go too high your sail will "luff" or begin to flutter and lose its taut shape. You'll feel yourself slowing down, and the pull on your arms will lessen dramatically. Bearing off slightly will remedy this.

Close Reach

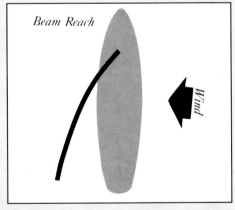

Beam Reach

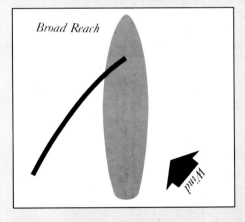

Broad Reach

2 A *reach* is sailing at a sideways angle to the wind. There are three variations; the *close reach*, the *beam reach*, and the *broad reach*. While reaching in light air is peppy and fun, reaching in strong winds is like going faster and faster down a ski slope; your margin for error gets smaller as you gain momentum. It's wet and wild!

On a *close reach* your sail should be sheeted out at roughly 30-

degrees from your board's bow-to-stern centerline, with mast angled slightly to windward. Direction of movement will be approximately 60-degrees off the wind. On a *beam reach* your sail should be sheeted out at 50 to 60-degrees from your board's lengthwise centerline; direction of movement 90-degrees off the wind (directly abeam). Mast should be angled somewhat further to windward than when on a close

reach. On a *broad reach* your sail should be sheeted out at roughly 70 to 80-degrees from the board's lengthwise centerline, with mast angled substantially to windward.

The sail and mast positions recommended here are start-point guidelines only. Weather and other variables will necessitate that you modify sail position, mast angle, and weight distribution according to individual situations.

DOWNWIND BOARDSAILING

Sailing downwind or "running" means that the wind is coming from behind you. On a sailboard, downwind sailing affects your stability more than with conventional small boats or catamarans.

Wind

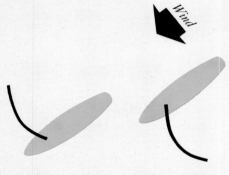

1 Bear away from the wind until you are sailing further off the wind than on a broad reach. Do this by tilting your mast forward and to windward. It will feel unnatural at first but it works. Keep lots of bend in the knees and elbows to initiate the bearing away maneuver.

2 As the wind moves from your side-rear quarter to behind you, shift your feet from their normal position aft to the daggerboard area, placing one foot on each side of the daggerboard well with toes roughly facing the bow of the board.

3 Ease the sail all the way out until it is open at a 90-degree angle to the wind. Maintain a course that keeps the wind coming from aft at a slight windward angle; the mast should be angled toward the windward-most influence. Both hands must move aft on the boom to prevent "rounding up" into the wind.

4 Steer by looking through the window in the sail and tilting the sail laterally from side to side for direction control. To veer left, tilt the sail right. To veer right, tilt the sail left. Allow your hands to move fore and aft on the boom as the demands of balance and steerage dictate.

5 Remaining stable is a matter of practice; as always, stay loose and allow your legs to be resilient. If the water's surface is unsettling due to chop or boat wakes—or if the wind is strong enough to cause difficulty—you can always drop one knee to the board or revert to a squat.

TACKING

All sailing craft must be able to change direction. There are two methods by which this is accomplished: 1) by pivoting the bow of the craft across the eye of the wind—*tacking*, 2) or by pivoting the stern of the craft across the eye of the wind—*jibing*.

1 Sail close hauled and angle the mast aft until the sail "luffs up" and the board turns well into the wind.

2 As the board turns into the wind and slows to a stop, release your sheet hand from the boom and grab the uphaul rope (or mast near the boom handle) while at the same time stepping forward and around the front of the mast.

3 As you step around the front of the mast, secure your grip on the uphaul by taking hold of it with your other hand (now a two-hand uphaul grip) and allow the mast to angle away from you somewhat.

4 This motion will lead you into swinging the sail across the stern of your board and stepping into your familiar starting position—but on the opposite side of your board!

JIBING

With the jibe, you begin by veering off the wind instead of into the wind as on a tack.

Wind

1 Leaning the mast forward and bearing away from the wind, assume a downwind stance (foot on either side of the daggerboard) as you begin to face dead downwind.

2 Transfering first your sheet hand to the uphaul and then your mast hand, allow your mast to tilt forward and sail to swing (weather vane-like) forward and around past the bow of the board.

3 Keeping your knees bent and back straight (as always), bring the sail all the way around to its new side and step back into your normal sailing position.

4 Reassume mast hand and sheet hand grip. Once again you're in a new direction and on your way.

5 As you practice this, try putting your weight on the rail opposite the direction in which you wish to jibe (leaning slightly rearward), lifting the bow somewhat. This will greatly accentuate your turning ability —especially in light wind.

BOARDSAILING SAFETY

SENSIBLE PRECAUTIONS

The sheer fun of boardsailing can cause some folks to overlook basic rules of safety. The fact that the wind is getting stronger or nightfall is advancing can easily go ignored when you're on the water and having a great time. But as so often reminded in these pages thus far, you're among the elements when on a sailboard and must use your head at all times. Reviewing briefly from earlier pages:

- Use the right equipment for your skill level and prevailing weather conditions.
- Wear the "right stuff" (wetsuit, harness, etc.) as necessary according to weather and water temperatures.
- Carry tools and spares sufficient to fix or replace faulty parts and "jury rig" if necessary.
- Utilize a mast-to-board "safety leash" so that in case of rig detachment the sail and board don't float apart.
- When sailing, don't go so far away from your point of origin that you're too tired to sail back. Use good judgement.
- Avoid sailing in complete isolation—so far from friends or other people that help would be impossible in case of mishap. Always let someone know your general whereabouts plan.
- Wear a life vest if you are a sub-average swimmer or if you intend on sailing any distance. Bouyancy assistance is a precaution basic to all types of boating.
- Respect the weather, study the weather, watch the weather.

GUARD AGAINST HYPOTHERMIA

Hypothermia, or "exposure" is the primary danger facing any sailor who spends an extended period of time on or in cold water. Beyond a certain point of physical exposure to chill air and water, body temperature can decrease rapidly, resulting in unconciousness. While immersed in water of 68-degree F, for example, a normal human body loses heat at over four times the rate as it does in air of the same temperature.

Getting stranded out on a large body of water due to increasing winds or nightfall is a matter of extreme risk. It all gets back to sailing within your limits, wearing and using the right gear, and keeping your whereabouts known. If you develop fatigue or excessive shivering while sailing, stop and go to shore!

SELF RESCUE

In the event of a rig breakdown or wind failure wherein further sailing is impossible, you must paddle or be towed back to shore. To accomplish this effectively, your rig must be compacted and out of the way so that you can paddle or be towed without obstruction or excess drag.

With board perpendicular to the wind as though prepared for uphauling the sail, position your rig (lying in the water) with mast facing downwind. From this position you can de-rig, roll up the sail and lash the boom to the sail and mast just as though preparing to carry the rig atop your car. When finished, simply lay the secured rig lengthwise (nose to tail) on your board. You can now "knee paddle" your board or be towed very effectively.

EXTRAORDINARY CIRCUMSTANCES

Drastic situations require decisive action. In the event of collision with another craft, get away and/or guard yourself from the point of impact any way you can. One of the rare cases when it is advisable to swim away from your board is if an unseeing skipper of a larger boat is going to run right into you. Sometimes there's no choice but to jump and swim fast and far.

Being stranded in deep water without help is really dangerous. No one should ever get into this situation, but it has happened. Being stranded in deep water without help in the cold is worse, and to get caught out after nightfall is worse yet. To combat hypothermia, actually de-rigging and rolling yourself in the sail helps shield the body from chill wind and pervasive moisture. Unfortunately this keeps you from sailing or paddling, but at least helps to physically re-charge for further action.

If the cause of being stranded is purely mechanical, i.e., a broken mast, boom, etc., "jury-rigging" is necessary. Without knowing the specific problem, recommendations are difficult to make here, however a damaged mast base, universal, downhaul, or outhaul

can all be lashed tightly with spare line, thus made to function. A broken mast is a larger problem. Generally you can re-piece a mast together by shoving the most tapered end into the wider end of whatever else is left. This leaves a shorter, yet functional mast from which to hang a sail and boom. Make it a habit to carry spare line and a utility knife on board if sailing any appreciable distance from the "home shore."

S.O.S.

If you need help from others, exhibit it by using the international request for assistance—arms outstretched and waving back and forth, one across the other. This is understood by an official Coast Guard, patrol, or knowledgeable boater.

RULES OF THE WATERWAY

- Keep away from port entrances or naval entrances that are heavily traveled by large boats.
- Never sail near swimmers
- Stay clear of moored boats
- Avoid powerboats.

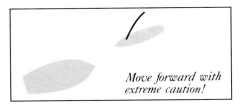

Move forward with extreme caution!

1. Technically speaking, a power-boat must always give way to a sailboard—but for your own safety—don't count on it!

2. If two boards sailing to windward are headed on a collision course, the board with wind on its port side (port tack) must give way to the boat on starboard tack.

3. A board going downwind must give way to a board sailing to windward.

4. If two boards on the same tack are sailing a collision course, the board furthest to windward must give way to the board downwind.

7 REGATTA!

You feel the fascination when you set eyes on a multi-colored fleet herding tight and fast toward the weather mark. "Could I be out there with those guys...?!" Sunlit sails overlapping, wind whipping them as they jibe, four sailors lose balance and fall like dominos, three burst speedily into the lead. The scramble that follows forms a moving string of beautiful prism-like colors.

A regatta is more than a race; it's feelings shared, effort given, and energy multipled. The atmosphere is cooperative and social, as opposed to the heated "win-at-all-cost" overtone of many competition events. The challenge of racing is demanding but fun, generating a go-for-the-gold standard of effort when a six-pack at the finish might be worth more than the prize!

Sailboard regattas began at a time when boardsailors were so few that getting together for a little wing-ding was the best way to keep in touch. Things aren't much different today; beginners and new board owners are welcomed to events and are urged to join local fleets. A typical regatta in sailboard style is an offbeat mix of hardy good times on the beach and bold competition in the water. Some folks go out to better their best, while others ply strategies to beat out the

pack and qualify for top seasonal events. Highest class honors hold space for few, but first finishers and last finishers go home ripe for the next go-round.

COMING OF AGE

Boardsailing is the audacious youngster of modern sailboat racing, following the Hobie Cat class in its fast worldwide growth and cavalier appeal. Bristling at conformity, yet respecting the legacy of traditional yacht racing, boardsailors are a class of "mustang sportsman" who sail not for the yacht club—but for the heart.

In any given hour of any given day, boardsailors are racing east, west, north, or south. In Connecticut, Rhode Island, the Carolinas, and Florida, boardsailors are racing while their Hawaiian counterparts are asleep. And when the Hawaiians are skipping white caps in the afternoon, sailors in Europe. Australia, Asia, and South Africa are in various stages of breakfast, lunch, dinner, and sleepy dreams. Sailboard racing is worldwide, bridging language and color and creed.

HUMBLE BEGINNINGS

Early boardsailing regattas started with Hoyle and Diane Schweitzer, close associate Alan Parducci, and James Drake, co-developer (with Hoyle Schweitzer) of the first modern sailboard. This tightly knit group was joined by an ever growing number of enthusiastic friends; some gatherings numbered only ten, others more than 25. Racing consisted sometimes of straight-line "drag race" duels, while other events were informal "around-the-buoys" affairs much like those of today— but with a bit less razzle dazzle. Boards used were handmade prototypes. It was hotrodding at its wettest.

In 1973, when the first polyethlene production boards were available through Windsurfing International, the first formal regattas began taking place in southern California. Originating in Marina del Rey, Long Beach, and Newport Beach, these quickly took shape as lively bashes that featured lots of healthy competition. Sailors brought their friends, regattas grew in size, and events spread to neighboring counties.

Early boardsailing regattas took place among the sport's creators and friends. Today's regattas vary widely in size, type, and locale.

In time, as boardsailing regattas went nationwide, individual dealers, various businesses and organizations began co-sponsoring events with the manufacturer and the "Windsurfer Class Association" was established. This was an organized body of the first boardsailing "one design" class. It formalized regatta activities by setting up a national program with four competitor weight classes and a standardized board and rig. The class borrowed precepts from the already popular "Laser" and "Hobie Cat" one design fleets, with rules and equipment designed for equal handicap among competitors. The groundwork for divisional fleets was initiated and a class newsletter was published.

A CLASS FOR EVERYONE

Today boardsailing regattas are held at local, regional, national, and international levels, with events of different types giving spice to the overall picture. "Funboard," "open class," "slalom," "one design," and "freestyle" all have aspects in common, but each is different from the other and many competitors tend to specialize. "Wave riding" is an event born in Hawaii; skills required for this event are extremely specialized and the accomplishments exhibited today are phenomena. Wave riding must be seen to be believed, and practiced seriously to be mastered.

Anyone with a board and basic skills can enter a boardsailing regatta. Local events—those once-a-week fleet get-togethers—are the best place to start. Beginners can enter One Design, Open Class, or Funboard regattas; which is best for you depends upon the preponderance of each type of event in your area and what type of board you have.

Fleet regattas are usually promoted by local boardsailing dealers. These contests form the backbone of organized racing in the U.S. and almost all well known skippers have received their training in these "home grown" ranks. There's a lot of volunteer effort in staging weekly (or monthly) fleet regattas; spouses, kids, friends, and work mates all chip in to make the program run smoothly. It's here that sailors are able to log the "board time in battle" that develops super sharp skills.

"TO BE, OR NOT TO BE"

How you progress up the ladder in regatta sailing depends on where you live and also the nature of your personal desire. Sun belt regions afford year-round regattas, thus allowing the luxury of continuous practice. In earlier years climate

and consumer interest made West Coast U.S. the hot bed for board racing; there were more sailors, more events, and more time to sail than in most other geographic regions. First world champion Bruce Matlack relates; "When a handful of Californians traveled to Bendor, France for the 1975 Windsurfer World Championships, we walked away with all top honors. The Europeans thought

Hawaii are unlike conditions in Michigan or Minnesota, and Gulf Coast conditions have variables not found in the Atlantic states. Importantly, it is very difficult to standardize the kind of experience or amount of expertise necessary to progress through the regatta ranks. It's a matter of going where the action is and seeing what happens. One thing's for sure: you'll always find out!

In the beginning, they may know little of class structure and less about rules. No matter. "Learn as you go" is a great teacher and keeps you having fun in the process. Don't fret about red tape and technical jargon, lest you come down with "paralysis from analysis!"

If you go to any sailboard regatta—especially the classic

our great success was due to physical training and lightweight boards and bodies—but our real key was California and years of practice in the diverse conditions there." Nowadays the Europeans set the standards due to more intense competition than in the U.S. over a wide range of European conditions.

California conditions are different than those of Hawaii, those of

Some folks aren't concerned with winning their class; they just love to get out and give it a go. Others are goal oriented and want to take the prize. There's plenty of room for either attitude in regattas large and small. Most people do not enter their first competition event with thoughts of top honors or visions of celebrated success in the distant yearly championships.

events that are held each year—it takes only a few minutes to see that points, rules, protests, and regatta management are important but secondary to the distinct flavor and special energy of each event. The time of the year, atmosphere, location, and participants are the elements that attract newcomers and veterans year after year. In ten different sailors you may find ten

different favorite regattas. Give racing a try and you'll soon find yours.

EXPLORING A NEW WORLD

Boardsailing regattas have a rhythm unlike traditional yacht club functions. They have an easier pace and are sort of molded to fit the weather on a given day. Most events are built upon the conventional "windward-leeward," or triangle course format. However more and more feature a mix of triangle course, one-on-one slalom, and a long distance race. Some even include a freestyle event. Points are tallied from the three or four events for an overall regatta performance score.

There is always a vast spectrum of performance at any regatta; often beginners tend their rigs on the beach right along side world

class experts. And that's the point. Those experts were beginners once— probably not too long ago. They learned from watching, listening, reading, and practicing. For novices and pros alike, sailboard racing never stops challenging skills, always provides opportunities for travel, and inevitably activates new friendships. In boardsailing, exposure is the soul mate of success.

ONE DESIGN CONCEPT

In sailboarding, the "Windsurfer®" class was the first and remains the largest One Design organization in the United States. Once established in the early 1970's, Windsurfer was recognized by the International Yacht Racing Union (IYRU), which gave it worldwide credibility and enabled operation under formal IYRU sanction. This achievement sped growth of the Windsurfer

class and helped spearhead sailboarding as an Olympic event, first featured at the 1984 summer games in Los Angeles.

The One Design format, which stipulates a particular size/weight/rig configuration for a craft, has long been proven as an excellent vehicle through which equal competition is achieved. Theoretically, if boards and rigs are of like size and configuration, then rigging knowledge, tactics prowess, and sailing skill will determine the winner.

In 1973, the first Windsurfer World Invitational regatta was held at Mission Bay in San Diego, California. The event featured a broad range of skilled and gritty competitors, along with much color and post race celebration. The following year's "Worlds," staged at Association Island, New York, brought the Windsurfer class to the East Coast in force and planted the seeds for future growth and popularity. Simultaneous development began taking place throughout Europe and by 1976 the class was on the road to super success.

The development of world championship events brought a new dimension to the Windsurfer class and an elevated goal for all com-

CLASS RACING

Above: European regattas are ebbulient affairs and are held in an array of beautiful settings.

petitors. The structure of the Class Association developed accordingly. Like others which are similar, the association is technically an owner's league that perpetuates and monitors class functions; primarily regattas and related events for points, benefits, and class promotion. In less than a decade the association has developed into a nationwide network of districts which are further divided into multiple local fleets. At this writing Windsurfer has eighteen districts, each with two to three dozen fleets.

Due to growth and an accelerating number of regatta contestants, a points system method of qualification for larger regattas (regionals, nationals, etc.) was developed. Now each district assigns an annual number of qualifying positions for the American Regional Championships. The number of qualifying positions are dependent upon the district's membership size. Each district schedules a minimum of five and maximum of ten "points" regattas per season. A contestant can qualify for the "regionals" by competing in a minimum of three

points events in a racing season. Off season "mid-winter" regattas and also local district championship events count fully as qualifying points regattas within the season that they are held.

THE ONE DESIGN CRAPSHOOT

Although by concept the sailor's skill determines success or failure in a given One Design race, other variables do enter the picture. Among them: 1) Lady Luck, 2) hardware.

In theory hardware in One Design is all the same. But the condition and state of tune of the board and rig are wild cards. Further, the

weight of the competitor as pertains to specific weather condition and rig tuning bears heavily on the success of anyone, skill or no skill, while on the course. Doing well requires a combination of good weather assessment, good board set-up according to you and your weight, and solid sailing.

Champion Nancy Johnson says it best: "there is always some pure luck involved in every regatta." When the wind is just the right strength for one person, it can be too strong for a fellow competitor of lighter weight—and yet it can be too light for someone in the same race who's big and prefers

heavy air. And Lady Luck plays a starring role here.

Optimum board speed varies with a particular wind velocity, contingent on just who is doing the sailing. You cannot always predict this variable before you leave the beach. It's just a fact in the game. Within certain limits you play the percentages. And that's the magnificent challenge of One Design!

OPEN CLASS

This category of racing is a direct result of growth and development in sailboarding. With the wide variety of boards and rigs introduced to the U.S. in recent years, no single product was necessarily the best or the most popular. Naturally there was on-the-bay competition between brands ("hey bud, bet my Flexi Whopper'll whup your Mega-Sprint— let's race!"). Thus "open class" racing among brands of similar design was instituted.

While brands other than the Windsurfer offer one design competition (chiefly Mistral and Wayler at this writing), neither of these classes are as widespread in the U.S. as Windsurfer and thus schedule fewer regattas in most areas. Open Class attracts brands from multiple classes; this results in a lot of regattas that are large and competitive.

The administrative body for Open Class in the U.S. is USBSA, the United States Boardsailing Association. USBSA divides Open Class into Division I and Division II, according to board type. Division I encompasses the wide spectrum of standard recreational boards, most all of which feature a flatter bottom and fit within certain established measurements. Division II covers the round-bottom family of board designs, those that are tougher to ride but have proven fast performers in triangle course racing. Division II board designs are an outgrowth of European light air lake racing, where testing and research have found round-bottom hulls effective, especially sailing to windward. The heat of European racing activity is on these types of boards, however flat bottom boards have proven more versatile and to date are more popular in the U.S. 1984 Olympic class boardsailing took place on the Windglider design, a a semi flat-bottom board type.

SPECIAL REGATTAS

OPEN CLASS OPTIONS

Equipment is a significant factor in Open Class racing. Skippers with sailing background in other classes generally take advantage of this, fashioning their rigs to best possible racing trim. You may use any mast preferred, providing it is of a circular mold (non-foil) and is not constructed with carbon fiber

material. Custom booms with special outhaul rigs may be freely used, in addition to sails and daggerboards desired. Sails and other components must meet weight and measurement rules. This leaves plenty of design latitude. Boards can even be handmade to your specifications, as long as they pass weight and measurement inspection at the event site.

PRO-AM AND PROMOTIONAL REGATTAS

Originally special events that were few and far between, both Pro-Am and promotional type boardsailing events are becoming more prevalent. In the case of Pro-Am, there are generally two types of events—those in which sailors use their own equipment and those in which boards

are supplied by the event sponsor/manufacturer. The latter makes for great competition, as highly skilled entrants all sail the same equipment and racing is a relatively pure test of individual skill.

But Pro-Am regattas are often invitational in nature, featuring "name" skippers from certain regions or only sailors that have earned their way to the event through points won in a qualifying series. Sometimes these regattas offer limited participation opportunity to average regatta sailors.

Promotional regattas are different. Often these are open entry regattas in which the manufacturer supplies the boards! The manufacturer's purpose in staging these extravaganzas is of course to promote a particular product. Often board manufacturers team up with automobile or other co-sponsors with compatible pro-

ducts and the result is an exciting "learn-and-race" day that attracts boardsailors of all ages and skill levels. These programs offer great opportunity for participants with little cost, no transport hassle, and none of the equipment entanglements of Open Class or One Design. You enter, show up, and race on the shiny new board of your choice.

At this writing the frequency of promotional events is spotty but on the increase. Most are one day "try-out-the-product" affairs, great for the experience but not scheduled every Wednesday or every weekend as in the established fleets and classes.

HIGH PERFORMANCE SAILBOARD RACING

There exists a whole spectrum within boardsailing of high performance regatta events which focus on specific skill disciplines. These events are wonderful to watch and truly challenging to participate in. Technically, competition falls into four categories: 1) "Funboard," 2) "Wave Riding," 3) "Freestyle," and 4) Long Distance. There are vast differences in the nature of these events.

FUNBOARD

This is the "unlimited" class of modern sailboard racing. The equipment is high tech, the racing is raucous, and the contests are wild. A typical Funboard regatta consists of a triangle race, a slalom event, and a thing called "ins-and-outs" which combines waves and flat water. Enter a Funboard regatta and you can expect one hell of a workout!

The Funboard class is an outgrowth of the annual Pan Am World Cup, the ultimate test for professional boardsailors worldwide. From the beginning, boards for this event had to handle high winds and waves, yet still function in relatively normal flat water course conditions. Equipment evolution and skill levels have gone completely "off the meter" during the Pan Am's development over the years, and like professional auto racing has resulted in a distilling of concepts into excellent hardware now available to consumers in the sailboard market place. Scaled down World Cup boards are now widespread, and lots of exotic production equipment is specifically manufactured and sold for this genre of racing. Although expensive, Funboard is a class wide open to new standards of equipment and sailing excellence.

Funboard regatta rules are simple: 1) a competitor must use the same hull throughout the duration of the regatta, 2) the hull must have its rig attached in only one place (free sail system). Sails can be modified or changed as desired, hulls can be custom made from high-tech materials such as Kevlar and carbon fiber for extreme lightness, and so on. Heavier sailors, those at a disadvantage in One Design, often prefer Funboard due to the compensating technical options (super light hulls, etc.) that can neutralize their body weight problem or even make it an asset. Keep an eye on the Funboard class; its primary popularity has been in Europe, but the U.S. version is on the rise.

WAVE RIDING

Here is something to look at closely—and try very carefully. Wave riding, or surf sailing events gained popularity in Hawaii and have now migrated to coastal regions of the continental U.S. Truly, this is a sport within a sport, so specialized and so magnificently unique as to attract fascinated eyes from people around the world. Much of boardsailing's celebrated visibility is the result of spectacular photographs of boardsailors in action on Hawaiian waves.

Wave riding events feature "wind-surfing" in its purest form—riders using the power of the wind to manipulate the moving force of waves. An incredible combination! These events are the most impressive to spectators because there is lots of action, usually quite close to shore. Regattas are usually professional or pro-am in format and are not for beginners. There is much drama, maximum skill demand, and always a danger factor. The forces of wind and waves are serious business.

Regattas consist of two event types: 1) wave riding/jumping, and 2) "ins-and-outs." Wave riding and jumping is judged subjectively on the basis of:

Transitions (smooth movement from wave ride to power jibe, etc.) as applied to a variety of maneuvers and the execution from one move to another.

Wave Jumping, including number of jumps and waves ridden, height of jumps, lengths of rides, wave face maneuvers, control, style and so on.

Ins-and-outs is racing in and out through the surf to pre-positioned buoys. Heats of four to six competitors are held in which the top one or two from each heat advance upward until a final heat is staged. Here, racers must be able to handle themselves in the surf and also sail speedily from mark to mark, plus *get around* each mark smoothly. Exciting to watch, tough to do.

Surf oriented regattas are critically dependent on both waves and wind, thus lean to Mother Nature for proper location and conditions. This factor alone will always limit the feasibility of wave riding events, so they will likely always be periodic and special.

Sequence footage of world renown Robbie Naish exhibits the marvelous "transitions" of wave riding. Naish "drops in" and "bottom turns", climbs to the top of the wave's crest and powers a "cut back", then drops back down the wave's face yet again to continue a lengthy ride and virtuoso performance.

AN EVENT FOR YOU

Freestyle is a sort of sailboard gymnastic event. Individual agility and imagination make this an athletic "personal expression" showing in which no two sailors' routines are the same. Judging is subjective, coming from a group of scoring panelists stationed at different vantage points. Each freestyle routine must start and finish within three minutes. This event, having undergone much growth and refinement, is extremely demanding for participants and a real pleasure for spectators.

Buoy Ball is a kind of crazy sailboard soccer. It is a light wind event played usually in teams of three-on-three or more. The ball used looks like a modified child's vinyl beach ball which incorporates a flexible ring for gripping with hand or foot. Sailors vie for ball possession with the objective of scoring goals. Ball possession is lost when an opponent sailor is able to touch, or "tag" the ball carrier's board. The result is a classic offense/defense tactical contest which involves strategy, teamwork, and guts. Great to play, great to watch!

Among the many special events uncommon to regular regatta schedules, *team racing* and *marathon racing* are of significant interest. Having originated in Europe, team racing blends triangle course racing together with three-on-three team tactics. The object, of course, is to win on a total team points tally over the opposing team. This involves fascinating coordination among expert tactical sailors, above and beyond that which occurs in boat-for-boat standard course racing. At this writing the best known sailboard team racing event in the world is the famous Sardinia, Italy regatta. This is an annual event which incorporates a kind of sailboard Mardi-Gras and invites

SPEED EVENTS

These are generally not categorized as regattas, however are increasing in frequency and should be mentioned. Speed events have to date been held for the purpose of record setting. Regattas for both have been held, however do not exist regularly at this writing. No doubt in time they will, as records connote competition, and the "dare" is always predessesor to the "do." Sailboarding is a "do" sport in its every aspect.

YOUR EVENT, THEIR EVENT

As mentioned, many regattas nowadays encompass more than one event type. *Triangle racing, slalom,* *freestyle,* and *buoy ball* are often packaged together in a single weekend's competition schedule. Each is unique and each requires specific skills.

Slalom racing is a wild kind of drag race with twists and turns. Contestants race head-to-head in pairs. Skippers must generate straight-line speed, make tight zig-zags through buoys, and achieve precise transitions from move to move. Among other hijinks that occur, sailors must cross each others' paths during the duel! Single and sometimes double elimination heats narrow contestants down to two finalists who race each other to determine the overall winner.

GET READY TO RACE

national teams from all over the world. National rivalry combines with all-out boardsailing to make an intense and festive event.

Marathon board racing is an optimum strength and endurance contest. Courses used may vary from multi-leg extended buoy layouts to coastal stretches from one town to another. Such races have measured up to 25 miles and are serious business. Like runners' marathons, they require supreme fitness, self pacing, attention to diet, and much mental fortitude. Marathons are staged at many large regattas around the world, and involve a wide spectrum of equipment and competitors, depending upon the regatta.

ENTERING YOUR FIRST REGATTA

Here's where it all comes into perspective. Preparing your sailboard for the rigors of competition ...packing and organizing for the trip to the event...arrival, sign-up and rigging for racing. The pieces of an adventure puzzle all fall crisply into place. Emotions are charged and your readiness finds its purpose.

The first thing you'll notice when you go to a regatta is that everything is scheduled. Sign-up in the early morning, skipper's meeting at 10AM or 10:30, first race before noon, lunch break, and then continued racing throughout the afternoon. If you prepare carefully,

you won't feel rushed. However, most boardsailors get behind the pace once in a while due to rigging adjustments or other details. Do the best you can and be ready for variables in weather and schedule. Always try to get in the water at least a half-hour before your starting time, as warm-up practice primes muscles and mind.

There are no formal prerequisites for entering a race, other than having a sailboard at your disposal. Needless to say, you should have some modicum of basic sailing skill under your belt. If you're a novice you'll be starting in beginner class. Things are a little more relaxed here than in the more advanced ranks where performance imperative is keen. Since beginners are just finding out what they can do, emphasis is more on finishing than placing.

BEFORE THE RACE

Get ready for the regatta *at home.* Registration must sometimes be in advance; if so, entry form and pay-

ment should be mailed as early as possible. Sometimes entry deadlines are firm and you can be left out of an event that has a limited number of spots for each class. This isn't always a problem, but it can be.

Organize your gear, pack any tools, spare line or fittings you desire, and keep your vitals in waterproof carry bags for dryness and transportability.

Racer Nancy Johnson strongly recommends one *large bag* for wetsuits, towel, sweatsuit, sail, daggerboard, harness, battens, and life vest. She then stresses the importance of a *small bag* for duct tape, hat or visor, sun glasses, sun screen, tools, spares, knife, lighter, wax, skeg and screws, beverage and snack. Check all gear off before depature; this will save many a "last-minute-stress attack" at the regatta site. It's the little overlooked details that cause most problems.

ARRIVAL PLANS

When race day comes, it's a good idea to get started early so you can

arrive in plenty of time to learn how things are being organized, who's staging the event and where the race course is. If you happen to be driving a long distance to reach the site of a regatta, it makes sense to go there a day in advance and stay in a motel or camp out. Most regattas are two day affairs and avid racers often equip themselves with van or camper rigs for frequent weekend junkets.

When you get to the beach in the morning, best thing to do is find a spot for your vehicle, get unloaded and move your sailboard to a location as near the shore as possible. The object is to provide easy launching and landing for your board and rig, since you'll be in and out of the water several times throughout the day.

As you get situated, learn where committee headquarters is. Sometimes it's a clubhouse or a trailer. Other times, it's just a well marked van or makeshift hut on the beach. Whatever its form, this is where you sign-up, pay your entry fee (if not done already), and get a course chart and racing instructions. Sign-up notifies the committee who you are, what weight division you're suited for, and what number you'll be carrying. Entry fee is a kind of administrative donation—usually a few dollars. Your sailing instructions normally include a course chart. Read these instructions carefully to familiarize yourself with the basic outline of the regatta and just how and

in what sequence it will be run. Course layout, marker locations, starting signals, and special flag signals will be explained.

Your course chart should be carried with you while racing so that you can refer to it as needed. While it's near impossible to drag the thing out of a wet shirt pocket while on course, many sails now come equipped with a clear vinyl chart pocket, afixed at the tack. This is handy and invaluable.

SKIPPER'S MEETING

Don't miss the skipper's meeting! As soon as you sign in, find out when and where the meeting is. This is a brief, informal orientation

held by the race committee for all entrants. Its purpose is to clarify the details of the event; where the starting line will be, the order of races, explanations of special signals, where to post protests, and all other pertinent information everyone must know. At the end of the meeting an ''official time'' is given, allowing all competitors to synchronize their watches with that of the committee. It's important to do this so you'll be matched with the official schedule and able to know exactly when your race starts.

If you have any questions at the skipper's meeting, raise your hand and ask them. Don't be reluctant; the only stupid question is the *unasked* question. If you wait until after the meeting and ask someone at random for information, you run the risk of an incorrect answer. If a heavyweight class contestant asks a lightweight contestant the first race starting time, the answer—however well intentioned—may be wrong because starting times for different weight divisions are not always the same. So get answers at best opportunity and from the most direct source.

RESPECT THE WEATHER

PREVAILING WEATHER

Three main elements comprise a "racing environment": 1) the course, 2) rival skippers, 3) weather.

The trick is to manipulate all three to your advantage. Weather is the most important factor. Everything else depends on it.

Find out about the weather ahead of time. Listen to the forecasts on radio and TV to get a general idea of predictions in the area where the regatta will be held. Look at newspaper weather reports; cut out and save local weather maps for a couple of days prior to the event and see what they indicate. Pay particular attention to the winds. Develop a "horse-sense" prediction of your own and compare it to the weather on site when you arrive. You'll be surprised at how accurate you can be—and how an educated feel for the weather will improve your sailing.

Also find out about the tides and currents where you'll be racing. For regattas being held in coastal bay or beach areas, the Coast and Geodetic Survey reports are accurate and helpful in their predictions of tidal flow. These reports are published in daily newspapers. If there is pronounced surface current or undertow on or near the race course, it will often be pointed out at the skippers' meeting. This is helpful, but always take it upon yourself to learn about any factor that will affect your boat movement once you're on the course and racing. It never hurts to converse a little with locals; fishermen, other sailors, harbor officials, lifeguards... anyone who will share a bit of local knowledge.

FIND THE COURSE

Assuming your boat is rigged and tuned to the best of your ability for the existing weather conditions, take a few minutes and really study your course chart. Absorb the information on it and orient yourself to the course layout. Next, scan the course, locate the committee boat and see if it has taken its position. Since it always moors near the start/finish line, it serves as a dependable point of reference. Now check your course chart and mentally match the real start/finish with the schematic drawing on the chart. This is your "nautical road map." Determine north, south, east and west; find out where you are in relation to your surroundings and in which direction you must sail in order to reach the starting area. Are there any channels where the current will be strong? Any shoals or other protrusions? Keep your senses alert to these things.

For wave riding regattas, find out where the judges will be sitting and station yourself in an area where you will be seen at all times. Study the wave patterns and breaker line

example: "A-B-C-D, round all marks to port" means just as it says—sail first to "A" mark, then "B" mark, etc., keeping the marks on your left as you round them.

for positioning. In surf slalom in large waves, sometimes the marker buoys bob in and out of view and you have trouble finding your way through the course. So careful observation ahead of time cannot be underestimated. A good strong mental note of just what's where is essential.

Having located the course area, you can quickly determine where the various marks are (there are usually three or four stationary marker buoys) by simply spotting them with the naked eye or binoculars. It's important to know one from another because you must round them in succession as designated by the race committee. For

COURSE NOTES

The basic course most often used in regattas is the "Olympic" triangle layout, or a variation of this. After learning just exactly what course you'll be sailing, find out how the race committee will inform entrants of a modified or shortened course, should this come into play. Generally notification will be made through sound signals in combination with the flying of a specific flag from the committee boat. At any time if you experience doubt or conflict here, remember that as a rule visual signals take precedence while on the water, written instructions take precedence on land prior to launch.

A PRACTICE RUN

Okay, it's time. You're ready to hit the water. One major item frequently overlooked at this juncture is warm-up. Plain 'ol stretches or calisthentics, whatever suits your style. Boardsailing is a very physical activity, and those muscles need some priming. More still, a short physical warm-up routine gives you a chance to mentally prepare and clear your mind of all things except the race.

If preparation is as planned, there should be time for a "tune-up" sail. Launch your board, sail out to the course area and acquaint yourself with the locale. This enables you to get a first-hand taste of the wind, currents, and landmarks in the area, plus test your board and rigging. Schedule enough time to sail the whole course and get a feeling for each mark rounding, the currents, and the day's winds. On returning to the beach you'll be familiarized with the area, physically stimulated and ready to make any necessary repairs or rigging modifications to your sailboard.

GET GOING

The committee boat will usually sound a rapid number of blurts from an air horn, signaling all competitors to sail to the starting area. But don't depend on a signal; use your own watch to tell you when to launch. (Incidentally, a waterproof watch is essential to racing. As stated at the beginning of this chapter, everything works on a time schedule. A watch is the focal point of your organization at the regatta). Doublecheck your gear, put on your life vest (and/or harness if necessary), and be sure your course chart is handy. You may want to keep a checklist of last minute tasks and run through it before leaving the beach. This isn't

essential, but many skippers do it just to keep the routine simple and avoid "over thinking" the details.

Races for the separate class levels (A, B, and C fleets), start at five minute intervals beginning with A-fleet. There are sometimes variations in the courses sailed by different classes, especially in Open Class racing. Pay close attention to these.

At the start of each separate race the committee boat will bear a flag showing which course to follow for your class. A glance at your course chart will clearly show where one marker is located from another,

Above: Set aside time for a practice run to learn the course, test the weather, and find your rhythm.
Top Right: Locate the starting line by sighting the "committee boat."

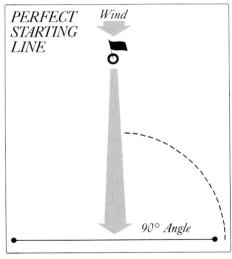

PERFECT STARTING LINE

Wind

90° Angle

according to the route you must follow. Commit this to memory if you can. Signal flags are shown as special numbers, letters or bright colors. A simple key is printed on most course charts which matches each special signal flag with its designated course. These are sometimes explained at the skippers'

meeting. The serious racer will commit all visual & sound signals to memory.

It makes good sense to carry a snack and beverage in your harness pack. Races are often run back-to-back (one right after another) with a rest period in between which is too short to allow a trip back to the beach. A cold drink and some quick energy food help bolster your stamina. And one frank recommendation: go easy on the liquids before a race; courses are not equipped with floating outhouses! If you gotta go, it's a makeshift procedure.

YOUR FIRST RACE

Don't worry about winning! Concentrate on finding out as much about racing techniques as you can, and above all have fun! To start your first race with even the slightest intention of winning

invites frustration. You'll learn more and enjoy the experience more fully if you work at skills in a natural stride.

OBSERVE THE OTHER FLEETS

If you are fortunate enough to have other classes starting before you, watch them. Observe how the individual boats jockey for their positions at the start. Pick one sailboard, watch it for awhile, then pick another. Compare the styles of the skippers. See if you can spot one that is more skillful and why.

Know exactly where the weather mark is from the starting line. If you cannot see it, watch where the boards in the other fleets go—and how they get there. By studying them carefully it's possible to see whether those at the starboard or port end of the line got better starts. Copy the strategy of the skipper you feel looks the most straight forward and effective.

WATCH YOUR MOVES

Take care not to observe so closely that you get in the way of people starting ahead of you. Sail clear of the starting line; this is an area reserved for the fleet that's on the "five minute gun" (next to start). Normally the starting line is marked with large, visible buoys at its boundaries. Move far enough away from the starting line and surrounding area so as not to cause interference...yet try to stay close enough to study what's going on. Careless interference may get you disqualified.

THE STARTING LINE

A perfect starting line is set at a 90-degree angle to the oncoming wind, perpendicular to both the wind and the weather mark. Theoretically, if two boats were to set

That is, go to the outside of either end of the line and sight straight down to the other end and line up with a distant landmark. This will give you a precise picture of the line from end to end, thus ensuring against going over early in the final rally for the start when the start marker buoys are usually obstructed from view.

You'll almost always be going to weather at the start, so prepare for a demanding "weather leg." When the ten minute gun sounds for your fleet, it's time to begin setting up your starting strategy. Getting a good start is great for the ego and crucial for winning races—but it's not essential to learning and having a good time. Do the best you can; keep your mind on your own plan of action and don't be disturbed by the presence of all the other boards.

STARTING PROCEDURE

When the five minute gun sounds for your race, look at your watch and begin counting half minutes. Be sure your watch is synchronized accurately with that of the committee. You should begin counting off whole minutes at the ten minute warning signal and as time nears

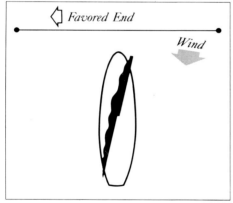
Favored End

Wind

out for the weather mark, starting at either end of the line—both boats would reach the weather mark at the same time after sailing exactly the same distance.

But wind, current, and surface variables make it very difficult to set up an ideal starting line. Most of the time there is a "favored end," one that is closer to the wind than the other. The common object of regatta sailors is to "find the favored end" and start from there.

FAVORED END

The most common "seat of the pants" method of determining which end of the starting line is favored is to position your board in the middle of the line heading dead into the wind. Let your sail luff and the boom will angle slightly, pointing in the direction of the favored end of the starting line. If the boom remains centered, you'll know the line is perpendicular to the wind and neither end is clearly favored.

THE START

At least a full ten minutes before the warning signal for your start time, you should be sailing around the starting area to ascertain the favored end. Once this is accomplished you can relax and begin getting ready on your stopwatch for the first of what are usually two signals before the start signal.

During this "pre-start" exercise you should also "sight the line."

the five minute preparatory gun, watch the committee boat closely to: 1) hear the sound of the gun (and see the smoke), 2) watch the signal flag being raised.

Importantly, the white signal flag will always be lowered exactly at either 30-seconds or 60-seconds before the five minute flag is raised. Sounds accompany the signal flags when raised—but not when they go down.

Start your countdown at the sight of the signal flag. (The gun will fire simultaneously, although the sound will be slightly delayed because of the distance between you and the committee boat).

Don't get behind on the countdown. It's a good idea to voice the numbers out loud: "five minutes to go...four and half minutes to go...four minutes...three and half" and so on. With one minute left count off every ten seconds and with ten seconds left

tick off one second at a time. Finally, START!

FIGHTING FOR CLEAN AIR

Don't wait to hear the gun before you sheet in for speed. You want to break away for "clean air" whether you've managed a good start or not. To do this, tack away from anyone shadowing you. Try not to tack too often though because the maneuver itself takes time and the lighter the wind, the more time it takes to tack. Once in clear air you can concentrate on board speed and negotiating the course as smoothly as possible.

If the fleet is heavily bunched up at the favored end of the line, often it's smart to start in the middle of the line or even down at the lee-ward end. This isn't necessarily slick strategy, but it side-steps the choppy water and conflicting air currents caused by congestion. This way you can concentrate on your

own board speed off the line with less interference from others.

How well you make your way from mark to mark will determine your ability as a regatta sailor. Even though there are other sailboards doing the same thing, yours is an individual effort. Spread your wings and worry about the details as you go. You'll fly fast and far!

THE RACE IS ON!

REGATTA STARTS

"over early" starter must wait for all other boardsailors to cross the line before re-starting.

The best way to prevent an early start is to cross the lien three or four seconds late. This isn't ideal but it serves as a good safety margin without causing too much inefficiency. Winners know, paradoxically, that if your're never over early you may never know how late you really are! The best skippers do in fact go over the line early occassionally.

REGATTA STARTS

There are several methods of setting up a good start for a race. Many competitors, however, make the mistake of getting fancy and not sticking to basics. The first basic rule of starting is: don't go over the line early. This puts you back much further than just being 5th or 8th or 12th over the line. Rules state that an

PORT APPROACH

Popular and precise. The port approach must be timed properly to work. First, choose a spot on the line that you desire according to whether or not there is a favored end. On to two minutes before the start, head along and below the line on a port tack. As you locate

your spot, immediately tack (you'll be on starboard with right of way) into position and get set to go.

Bear in mind: 1) all boats to leeward of you have the right of way; interference with them risks disqualification for "barging," 2) try to keep 1-2 board lengths between you and the next racer to leeward so you can get into a reach and gain speed just seconds before the start, 3) try to avoid the "bad air" of others near you.

LUFF START

The easiest and most basic start. Pick a spot along the starting line and ease in just windward of it, luffing your sail. This leaves you sufficient room to drift to leeward. If the line is crowded, don't get too "high" on the line because a leeward boat can "luff you up." Keep an eye on prevailing current, as this can affect your drift. When the start gun sounds, just sheet in and go!

DIP START

Takes practice, judgement, and nerve. As though crowding in line, you approach the starting line from a position in front of the other boats, finding an open spot among them and "dipping in." A good dip start provides great acceleration but runs the risk of fouling other boats; it's like threading a needle.

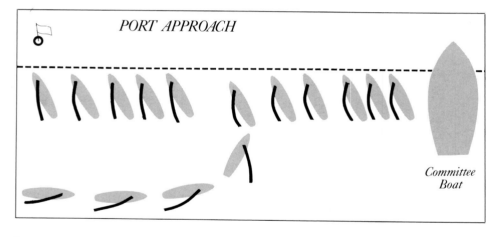

PORT APPROACH

Committee Boat

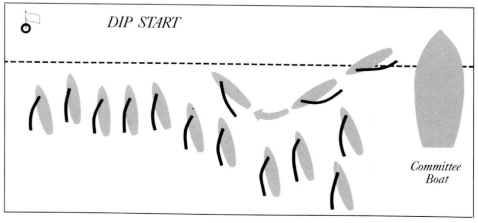

DIP START

Committee Boat

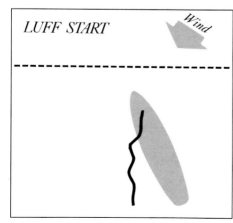

LUFF START

Wind

BASIC REGATTA RULES

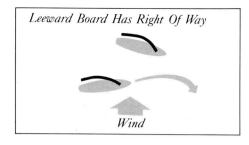

LEEWARD BOARD

The windward board must give way in all but two situations: 1) when two boards are rounding a mark and the windward board is on the inside, 2) when a leeward board is overtaking from astern on a free leg of the course and fails to maintain parallel until clear ahead.

OVERTAKING

A board moving up on the rear of another board on the same tack must stay clear of the board ahead. When an "overlap" is established (see terminology chart), the leeward board rule comes into effect.

SEA ROOM (same tack)

(Also known as 'Room at the Mark') If two or more boards (on the same tack) are rounding a mark, the board on the inside has the right of way if it can establish an overlap. Otherwise, the board on the far outside has the right of way—if it can establish an overlap.

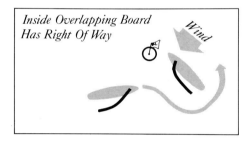

SEA ROOM (opposite tack)

(Also known as 'Room at the Mark') A board on starboard tack has the right of way over a board on a port tack. However, on a downwind leg the inside overlapping board has the right of way at a mark—regardless of tack.

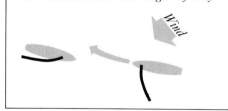

SAME TACK

If two boards on the same tack are on a collision course, the close-hauled board has the right of way. Boards sailing downwind must stay clear of boards on the same tack which are pointing.

TACKING/JIBING

A board in the process of tacking or jibing must stay clear of any board making headway on port or starboard tack. If two boards are tacking simultaneously, the one to the port side of the other must stay clear.

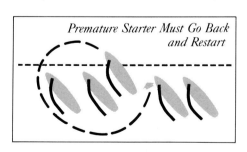

EARLY START

Any board that goes over the line before the gun fires must sail clear of the fleet and, when the opportunity permits, move back behind the line and re-start.

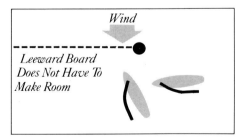

CONTROL BARGING

When negotiating for the start, a leeward board does not have to give room to a windward board trying to "barge" its way in front of the leeward boat to accomplish a legal start.

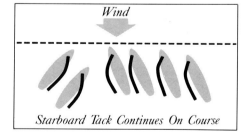

STARBOARD TACK

Starboard tack has the right of way over a port tack board. You're on starboard tack when the wind is blowing over your right side (starboard side). A board on port tack must steer clear of a starboard tacker's course.

8 PERFORMANCE & SURFSAILING

Butterflies in your stomach, you work gingerly to prepare your rig for launching. Wind is more than a breeze at your back; white caps are forming on the seas in the distance and the steady blow is interrupted with aggravating gusts. While adjusting your footstraps and rubbing a thin coat of wax on the board deck for secure footing, you scan the horizon. Twelve knots of wind. In an hour it'll be fifteen. Taking care that your lightweight board and sail don't fall sideways to the wind, you lift and position them precisely, lest they blow away in a gust.

Entering the water with sail on your head and board at your side, before even waist deep you lower your board and set the mast in its perpendicular position. In a single motion it all happens. Wind fills your sail, you're hoisted rapidly into a standing position and with a sudden burst of soundless force you're fast, fast, fast on the move!

With wind in your hair and spray in your eyes, all sights are a blur, all judgement becomes sensory. Board skittering over the surface and sail full of invisible power, you're in vertical flight—disconnected from the land and unplugged from the world. This is performance boardsailing— another dimension!

SPEED, WIND, AND MAGIC

High performance sailboarding is an ever advancing "sport-within-a-sport," both in terms of equipment and skill standards. Boardsailors try new things, equipment is pioneered to enable more demanding maneuvers, new maneuvers lead to still newer equipment, and so on. A fascinating, healthy development is the result.

While modern performance boardsailing has become associated (through the media) with the ultra short boards, high aspect sails, and winds of Hawaii, plain old skill is what fires the sport along and as such applies to any size board. Advanced high performance boardsailing takes place on all kinds of boards; sailors and the weather are what make it all happen. Fancy equipment helps it happen better.

STRONG WIND TECHNIQUE

Performance boardsailing requires wind—more wind than simple recreational sailing. A large part of advanced learning is basic mastery of strong wind conditions. With a wind strength of above 12-mph (about 8-9 knots), you enter a new world of boardsailing sensations. This is a harsher, yet more exciting experience.

Getting uphauled and under way in strong winds is actually tougher than sailing itself. At first, it's downright frustrating. Uphauling the sail against a gusty wind makes balance difficult, causing a forward fall—usually many forward falls. Or you finally get the sail up and either sheet in between gusts or round up into the wind. Either results in a backward fall.

PAYING YOUR DUES

Following is a list of pointers that will help speed up the strong wind learning process. Notice that the list begins with uphauling—the biggest hurdle.

- Uphaul quickly, keep knees bent and back straight. Leverage yourself with the strength of your thighs and your body weight. Get the sail completely out of the water and get set to sheet in and go quickly.
- You'll need more than arm strength to sheet in and keep your balance. Quickly tilting the mast well to windward (sail not yet sheeted in), lean well back into the wind and then immediately sheet in. You will feel as though falling backward into the water but as you sheet in the wind will suspend you and you'll be rushing forward in a flash. Needless to say, the timing and coordination of this procedure requires practice and involves lots of falls before success is achieved.
- Keep footing and weight outboard and aft of normal; just how far aft will come naturally with practice.

HIGH SPEED STABILITY

Inevitably, speed becomes the addiction of the advanced boardsailor. But speed is achieved with skill—not just strong wind and raw nerve. When sailing a standard long board downwind or on a reach in winds over 15-mph, daggerboard "lift" becomes so effective that the board tends to "plane-up," riding first on its leeward rail and then on the windward rail. A side-to-side oscillation takes place which is rather exciting! Modern short boards have circumvented this by eliminating the daggerboard, whereas most modern standard and funboards now have retractable centerboards, adjustable up or down with a foot lever. Long boards without retractable centerboards require hand operation for both retraction and insertion.

HOLDING A PLANE: SHORT BOARD SAIL AND BOARD TRIM

Once you've had a few speed runs on a short board with high aspect sail, you'll be amazed at the ease of screaming reaches and at how fast a sailboard can actually go. The key to fast sailing is trying to keep your arms and legs stiff so you don't absorb the power of the sail in your body. Instead, you transmit it right into the board for speed. Also, it is important to constantly be trimming your sail for maximum power. You should fill the sail with just enough wind to eliminate wrinkles and no more. Over-sheeting will cause you to spill wind, just as luffing the sail causes you to go slower. Keeping the board flat—even healing it over slightly to leeward will also help maximize your speed. Both foot placement and the amount of pressure on the sail are also relevant to wind speed. The faster you go, the further aft you must stand to counterbalance the pressure of the sail on the nose of the board.

SHORT BOARD, LONG BOARD

THE PERFORMANCE WIZARDRY OF MIKE WALTZE

An early pioneer of performance boardsailing on waves and flat water, sailor/board builder Mike Waltze is foremost in skill and style. His excellent book, "Performance Sailboarding," describes and dissects the fascinating techniques that can transform a recreational boardsailor into a performance master. In this chapter, Waltze overviews the equipment, principles, and basic skills necessary to successfully enter the dynamic world of sailboarding at the high performance level. His words are wise and his experience is unsurpassed.

HIGH-TECH PERFORMANCE

Today's performance boardsailors thrive on speed and board handling. Carving jibes, riding waves, getting airborne, and blazing across the water at high speed are what more and more sailors are becoming able to do. To attain this kind of performance, proper equipment is essential. This equipment must be well suited to the sailor, it must be "tuned" properly, and it must be used for what it's designed to do. Fortunately the equipment is avail-able. Not such a short time ago, high tech boards and rigs simply didn't exist. Now that they do, fantastic things are possible.

The primary equipment difference between performance boardsailing and standard boardsailing is the board. True performance sailing requires a shorter, very different "stick." This includes eliminating the daggerboard, modifying the "plan shape," fashioning the rails differently, and—of course—finding a mast, boom, and sail that coordinate with the board. The "short board" relies solely on either a single fin or tri-fin design to achieve lateral resistance (keep the board from sliding sideways). Techniques necessary to operate this contrap-tion are in many cases quite opposite those that most boardsailors are used to. And yet sometimes they're simpler. Hopefully this will become clear as we move along.

BREAKING THE BARRIERS

It is well known that the original standard Windsurfer was more than demanding to sail in winds over 15 knots. The development of high-wind daggerboards assisted board control in this kind of wind velocity. However, even with better control you still had to hold on! Invention of the conventional harness was a big help here; it relieved most of the severe tension on the arms and allowed for comfortable high wind sailing.

Then footstraps came along. Sailors could stick to their boards in battering surface chop and when flying over waves! With streamlined daggerboards, plus harnesses and footstraps, whole horizons of experimentation opened up for boardsailors who dared to seek the outer limits of performance. Sophisticated skills created the demand for faster, more maneuverable boards. With the advancement of sailboards came the advancement of sails and components. Better equipment has opened the doors to feats undreamed of.

THE RIGHT STUFF

For a high performance "short board" to work, you need wind.

And plenty of it. This is often the first thing that scares away an interested sailor who is accustomed to a 12-foot board. But surprisingly, it's easier to sail a short board in 15-18 knots of wind than in 10-knots. In Hawaii, for instance, a person who learns on a short board feels completely awkward on a standard board and in fact sometimes can't even steer the thing in 10-knots!

For you, where you'll be sailing and what you want to achieve has an important impact on your choice of equipment. And your equipment is critical to your success; it can make your first short board experience a nightmare or a dream come true. So let's do some analysis with "the three W's": the amount of wind you'll be sailing in, the type of water you'll frequent (lake, ocean, surf, etc.), and your personal body weight.

THE SHORT BOARD

First, an overview. Most often, the best board for a first-time performance sailor is a full "floater," one that allows uphauling the sail without the board sinking beneath your feet. Heavy sailors—those in the 200-pound range will need something around 10-feet in length, whereas someone in the 125-pound range can get away with an 8 to 8½-foot board. For sailing on lakes or in small waves in light to moderate air (12 to 18 knots), an average board for an average sailor of 150 pounds would fare well with the following dimensions: 8-feet 6-inches in length, 22 to 23-inches in width, 13-inches of nose width (measured 12-inches back from the nose tip), and 14-inches of tail width (measured 12-inches from the tail). As you shop around for a board, you'll find great variation in the custom and production molded short boards. Those of similar length and width measurements don't always have the same shape—and when measurements start to vary, shapes become extremely different from one another.

BOARD LENGTH

A longer board will float better and is more practical in light to moderate wind. A longer board will take a little more effort to turn and will be a little slower to respond than a shorter board, particularly in the surf. In turns, the longer board will "plane out" quicker in lighter air, but will be slower in strong wind due to its excess drag. A smaller board is more of a hotrod. It's responsive across the spectrum —turning, transitions from one move to another, and top speed. But the short board requires more wind and a higher degree of skill to be any fun.

BOARD WIDTH

A wider board serves the purposes of holding and initiating a "plane" more easily than a narrower board. This is due to the increased area of wetted surface, which allows for ample flotation. It makes light-to-moderate air sailing more enjoyable, allowing quicker responsiveness.

However, for high winds and effective high wind sailing, it is essential to reduce board width and employ a narrower outline shape. This reduces the amount of curve in the rail line; the board is then more controllable at high speeds (though difficult to turn at low speeds). 200-pound Fred Haywood used an 8-foot, 6-inch, 18-inch wide Sail-boards Maui board in his record breaking 1983 speed run of over 35mph.

BOARD NOTES

A general rule of thumb is that a board should only be as long as is necessary to initiate a "plane" in a given wind and keep planing (not sinking or pushing water). The shorter the board, the faster you will go because of less drag and less weight. A board should also be only as wide as you need for your given weight and the predominant conditions you sail in. A board that's too wide makes for difficulty in sinking the rail and controlling a turn when jibing in strong winds. Most Waltze personal boards are only 19½ to 21½-inches wide (Mike weighs 130-pounds), while in comparison Fred Haywood sails 22 to 24-inch wide boards in the same conditions. His 200-pound weight makes the difference.

If you try a board and can't control it properly in strong wind, it's most likely too long, too wide, or has too much curve in the rail line for the speeds you're reaching. The opposite would be true if the board were sinking under your feet.

TAIL SECTIONS

A basic tail is a rounded "pintail." A "winger" pintail (see chapter 9) is used to reduce tail area without narrowing the curve in the overall outline shape of the board. A "swallow tail" provides increased tail area yet keeps the tail curve relatively straight, reducing a wider board's tendency to spin out at high speeds. A "pintail" is essentially a more pointed version of the rounded pin; it is used mostly on very narrow boards with minimum tail curvature. The "diamond tail" is sort of a compromise between a swallow tail and rounded

pintail. An "asymmetrical" actually combines two tails on one board. It is used specifically for wave riding where you need a narrow board and tail for fast bottom turns and a wider board and tail for cutbacks during deceleration.

RAILS

The rail contour on a short performance board should be nicely foiled; not too fat or too rounded. A "boxy", or roundish rail is good for light air but difficult to control in strong winds because it doesn't slice the water as effectively as a well foiled rail. A "pinched" rail is the most efficient for high wind sailing in general, however for heavier riders a fatter rail offers better control.

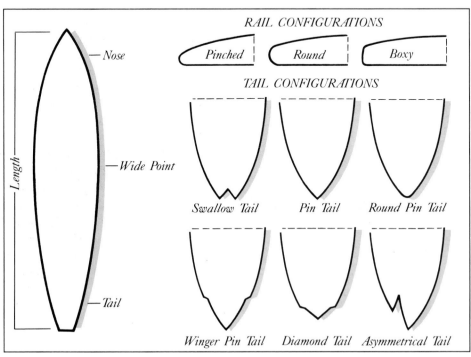

Nose

Wide Point

Length

Tail

RAIL CONFIGURATIONS

Pinched   *Round*   *Boxy*

TAIL CONFIGURATIONS

Swallow Tail   *Pin Tail*   *Round Pin Tail*

Winger Pin Tail   *Diamond Tail*   *Asymmetrical Tail*

FIN CHARACTERISTICS

Without fins, a short board would simply slide sideways and never be able to go in a straight line. In all cases, a calculated amount of "skeg area" is necessary to control side-slipping, known as "crabbing" or "cavitation."

Generally, a single fin arrangement allows for optimum responsiveness, but cavitation is reduced with the increasingly popular tri-fin designs. So each set-up has pros and cons. Three-fin boards offer the best stability, and in light winds tend to glide smoothly through turns. They also don't require as much precision in foot placement and pressure on the tail. But for lighter weight sailors, a single fin board's sensitivity enables better control in high winds—and it turns with quicker responsiveness.

In light-to-moderate air performance sailing spots, you'll likely see many wider tail, wider outline, three-fin sailboards. At a super high wind, high speed spot such as Hookipa Beach Park (Maui, Hawaii), you'll see more narrow outline, narrow tail, single fin boards.

BOARD CONSTRUCTION

The options here, for all practical purposes, are roto-molded plastic, ABS plastic, and custom-shaped polyurethane foam skinned with fiberglass. Production plastic boards have the advantage of being the most durable and having the longest life. But these are heavier and lack the detail perfection in rail shape that's available in good custom boards. To good sailors, this means less responsiveness. And fiberglass boards carry the advantage of being custom designed for your own weight and sailing ability. Not to mention their beautiful appearance. But a fair warning: fiberglass boards aren't cheap and they are much more subject to damage than durable production boards.

THE RIG

A performance board is only as good as the rig will allow (mast, boom, and sail that goes with it). A performance rig is basically a high aspect sail that has a higher clew and shorter booms than the sail with which most people learn. The narrower profile is designed to handle higher speeds, aiding control and making the most of the wind's power. From a practical standpoint, the design also helps keep the boom out of the water during low angle turns and jibes. The mast for this type of sail is much stiffer than standard, reducing sail distortion. The stiffness also ensures that the power of the wind isn't absorbed by the bending mast—that it is instead fed right

into the board to create instant acceleration and speed. The sail design is much flatter than for, say, a light air racing or freestyle sail. And draft is much further forward, making it easier to hang on and stay in control through gusts. Serious performance sailors own two or three different sail sizes to be able to sail in a variety of winds. It's no fun being under or overpowered by the wind.

RIGGING POINTERS

Prior to sailing, it's vital that your high performance equipment be rigged properly. Otherwise it could be inefficient or even unsafe. Sufficient downhaul must be placed on the sail to keep the draft forward. Outhaul adjustment should be a balance—not too full or too flat. A tendency toward fullness is better for lighter winds, while a flatter sail is necessary for very strong winds. All lines should be checked for fraying and there should be no sharp edges on your skegs, footstrap screws and other protrusions.

PREPARE TO LAUNCH

Adjust your footstraps so your toes can just barely be seen sticking out from the strap. A loose fit is dangerous. One nice advantage of a short board is that it's easy to carry. This is done by using your sail a bit like a wing and sort of letting it carry you to the water (see photos). With sail in a horizontal position and the length of the mast perpendicular to the wind direction, the board should be a bit to windward of the tip of the sail. Pick the board and rig up from the windward side—the mast with your windward hand—your grip at the tack patch. Lift the sail atop your head while picking up the board with your free hand by gripping a footstrap. You can then easily walk to the water with board and sail balanced.

Once at the water, set the board down, sheet in on the sail and... you're off! (Needless to say, the water must be deep enough for your skegs to clear and you must jump onto your board as you sheet in).

WATER START

The most efficient way to begin sailing a short board is to water "water start." This is accomplished when the board and sail are lying in the water and you use the wind to lift body and sail out of the water and onto the board.

To water start, situate your board so that it is perpendicular to the wind, with the mast to windward of the board. The sail's clew should be pointed in the general direction of the board's tail. It pays to get the board and sail into position quickly, as the mast sock will retain air and float the rig for a short time, making it easier to pop the rig out of the water and get going.

Start by swimming out to the mast tip to gain the necessary advantage needed to free the clew from the water. This can be achieved by shaking the mast head vigorously until the booms are clear from the water, then "hand-walking" back down the mast. Keep your front hand above the booms until you are well situated and ready to start. Now grab the booms with both hands (forward hand on the mast below the booms in lighter airs) and get at least one foot up onto the board. In this position you will be able to steer the board just as if you were sailing. Do this by tilting the mast aft to head into the wind, and forward to bear off the wind. When you are in the beam reach position, hold the sail as high as you can, wait for a puff, and let the sail pull you up onto your board.

Try kicking with one foot if you find it difficult to get out of the water and onto the board. With a little practice and help from friends, this awkward and seemingly impossible maneuver can become second nature.

BEACH START

Launching a sailboard from the ocean shore is a skill all its own, especially when traversing "shore-break" waves or a strong sideshore current. Uphauling in these conditions can result in broken gear, embarrassment, or even injury. Learning to beach start can be a good introduction to learning to water start, and it is a necessary endeavor for anyone who wishes to boardsail in the waves.

Prepare for a beach start by positioning your board in shallow water, just deep enough that the skeg will clear bottom when you jump on the board. Point the nose of your board so that it's perpendicular to the wind direction (as though you were sailing on a beam reach). Grab the mast with your front hand, and the boom with your back hand (both hands on the boom in heavier air). The board will probably want to round up (turn into the wind) as you attempt to jump on. Preventing this takes practice and concentration on a few key details.

Stand close to your board so that it is nearly in contact with your legs; don't attempt to sheet in hard before you're ready to sail or actually sailing. "Steer" the board to a reaching position before stepping on by pushing with your forward hand on the mast (you may hold the mast well above the booms as you position the board just prior to stepping on).

Finally, step on quickly (most people step on front foot first) and immediately bear off (pressure on the leeward rail with aft foot, sail forward) to a solid, stable reach. Remember that you can often regain control if you become overpowered or "out of shape" during this maneuver by simply sheeting out a bit with your sheet hand.

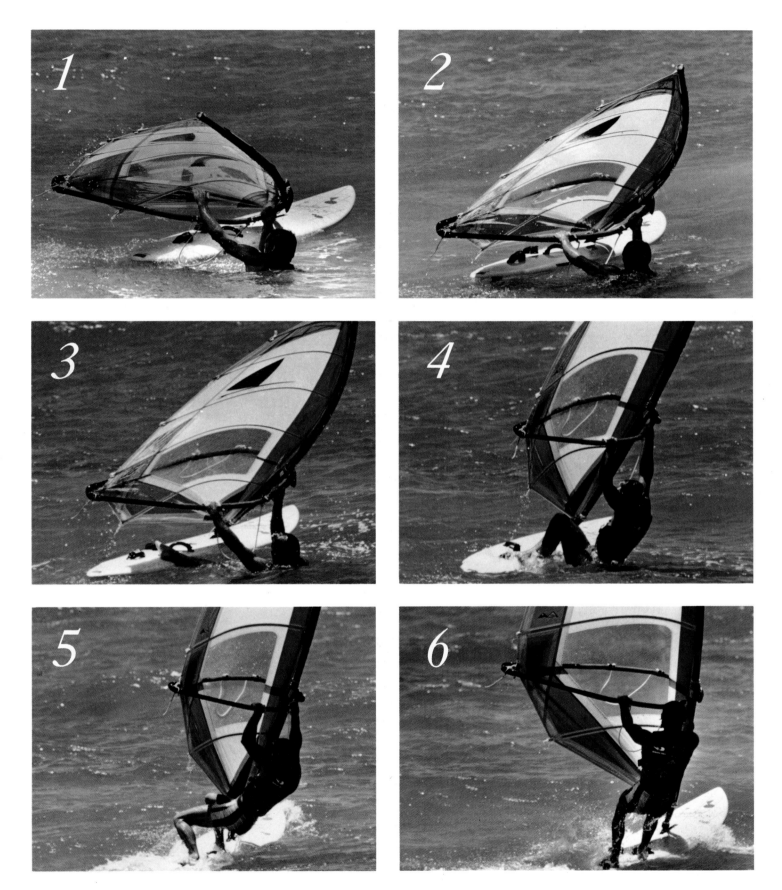

CHANGING DIRECTION

Tacking, jibing, and bearing off in strong winds require speed, physical agility, and some strength. Even bearing off, the least extreme of these three basic maneuvers, is considerably more difficult than in lighter winds. When bearing off from a reach to downwind, for example, the sheer power of the wind on the sail is stronger than you and can rip the sail from your hands or launch you forward into the water. To avoid this, crouch slightly and sheet in and out while bearing off so as to graduate the sail's power load.

FAST TACK

Performance boardsailing generally requires that you come about, or change tacks rapidly—both to aid balance on the board in choppy water and to get around marker buoys quickly while racing. In light air sailing, tacking is a delib-erate, slow motion, but in strong wind the motion must be quick, smooth and efficient.

HIGH PERFORMANCE JIBES

As with tacking, advanced sailboard jibing must be done quickly and precisely. While there are a wider range of jibe movement variations than found in tacking, a running jibe is the most basic advanced jibe done on long boards ("floaters") and a power jibe is the most popular and effective for short board sailing. There are many other jibe variations, including the flare jibe and duck jibe (see page 136).

LONG BOARD FAST TACK

SHORT BOARD FAST TACK

1 Raking your mast well aft so as to head up into the wind rapidly, move forward on the board, front foot ahead of the mast base and mast hand moving from the boom to the mast just below the boom-to-mast connection.

2 Passing bow-first through the eye of the wind, step around the front of the mast, now gripping the mast with your prior sheet hand and letting go of it with your mast hand.

3 Completing your movement around the front of the mast, sustain your grip on the mast and allow mast-and-sail to angle forward as you grab the boom with your free hand.

4 Now lean back, repositioning yourself with both hands on the boom and feet in place for your new tack.

RUNNING JIBE

Essentially a speeded up basic jibe (see chapter 6), this jibe requires that you bear off the wind until your stern passes through the eye of the wind, after which a simple mast/boom hand transfer assists the sail around. As the board changes direction, you adjust foot position to the opposite side, reassume boom grip (same as before except that the mast hand becomes sheet hand and vice versa) and head off on your new point of sail. The difference between a basic jibe and a running jibe is that a basic jibe is controlled through gripping the uphaul or front boom handle, whereas a running jibe is controlled by moving the hands along the boom, accentuating mast rake to windward, using some foot and body english.

POWER JIBE

Necessitating good footwork and hand-eye coordination, the power jibe allows a super-fast direction change because you maintain good speed throughout the maneuver. On a short board, the power jibe is a kind of speedy carving motion in which sail manipulation is almost effortless. On a long board you must forcibly push the sail outward ("back the sail") and around to the opposite side of the board and then jerk it back into position for your new direction—maneuvering the board compatibly with your feet and weight in the process! Motion makes it easier than it looks, but it still takes lots of practice. Pictured here is a long board power jibe demonstrated by Jeff Miller, and Mike Waltze demonstrates a classic

HIGH PERFORMANCE JIBES

short board power jibe on page 139.

FLARE JIBE

Sometimes considered a jibe for high wind, the flare jibe is based upon getting your weight low and aft so as to sink your board's tail and pivot around on the fin. Approach and execute this jibe essentially as with a running jibe, stepping back as you bear off and pivoting the board into its new direction with your feet as the stern passes the eye of the wind and your sail whips around. Rail control is critical when doing this in choppy conditions, especially on a long board when the daggerboard is in the down position.

DUCK JIBE

The duck jibe is a method of fast jibing, dynamic in theory but generally not as fast as a power jibe. This jibe is used in short board wave sailing, as well as in long board freestyle routines.

Begin your duck jibe by applying weight and pressure on the downwind rail while planing on a reach. Bearing off of the wind, lean into your turn, keeping your sheet hand well aft on the booms. As your stern nears the eye of the wind, stretch your arms back and actually throw the booms up, over, out and away from your head! As the sail passes through the wind's eye, switch your foot positions on the board quickly and catch the booms with your hands. Sheet in, adjust your position and balance, and away you go on your new tack.

Once again, all this falls into place under the forces of motion.

Far Left, Top Sequence: Running Jibe
Far Left, Bottom Sequence: Long Board Power Jibe
Below, Top Sequence: Flare Jibe
Bottom Sequence: Duck Jibe

SHORT BOARD POWER JIBE

TURNING AND JIBING

Turning on a short board at high speed is one of the greatest thrills you'll experience (after recovering from the speed sensation). Unlike a long board with a daggerboard which must be turned like a boat, a short board is maneuvered like a surfboard or water ski by leaning the board into the turn and sinking the rail. You actually carve the board by putting pressure with your back foot on the rail in the direction you wish to turn. Little

sail movement is necessary. Going out of control at high speed is no longer a worry and jibing becomes a thrill instead of a nightmare.

To perform a jibe on a short board, begin by turning away from the wind and continuing all the way through, drawing a 180-degree arc until you are on the opposite tack. To prepare for a jibe, get in a comfortable sailing position, take your back foot out of the footstrap and place it just in front of your aft strap on the leeward rail. Add pressure with your back foot, and as your board begins to turn, trim your sail so that it remains full of wind but not oversheeted. In moderate air, just as you've passed the downwind position, release your sail with your back hand as you continue carving the board all the way around. If you stop carving or applying pressure with your back foot, the board will stop turning and you won't complete the jibe. Try to time the release of your sail so that as soon as your board is pointed on a beam reach off the new tack, you are just sheeting in on your sail. If you release the sail too early, your sail will come around faster than your board and you won't complete the jibe. You will be launched over the nose of your board. If you release too late, your board will precede your sail around and you will find the nose of the board pointing straight into the wind. You'll be in the water by the time your sail comes around.

In light air, because your board will be moving slowly, it is necessary to wait longer before you release your sail. In strong winds, the opposite is true and you'll find it necessary to release the sail before you reach the downwind position so that your board and sail meet in unison on the new tack and you don't lose any speed.

WAVE RIDING

SURFSAILING

Dropping down the face of a wave on a sailboard is much like dropping down that first hill of a roller coaster. Your stomach sort of leaves your body and stays a few feet behind you, and doesn't catch up until the ride ends. What an exhilarating feeling! Or if the elevator goes down too fast—that same sensation of the foundation falling out from under you, of weightlessness. The forces of nature are giving you one heck of a thrill ride, as exciting as any roller coaster. And the best part is that you can keep experiencing the thrill over and over again, as long as your energy holds out.

It's one thing to drop down the face of the wave, but to cut back up and ride it down again takes the thrill to an even higher level. Feeling the momentum of the wave, going with its flow, being one with its power, provides a feeling that's almost indescribable. You're part of one of nature's strongest forces: the sea—and the waves that roll from her.

Then there's going the other direction—out through the waves, jumping them—finding yourself ten feet in the air! Again, that feeling of weightlessness as you fall back down to the water—that feeling of free falling from space. You land just in time to get ready for the next wave, for the next flight.

Playing in waves takes the sport of sailboarding to a highly exhilarating level. It takes a higher level of expertise, coordination, and physical fitness. It's certainly not for everyone, but for those who must take things to the ultimate limit, surfsailing is that limit in sailboarding.

FITNESS

For those of you contemplating your readiness for this stage of the sport, let's talk a bit about physical training. Surfsailing takes much more strength and stamina than regular flat water sailing. One should be in good physical shape. Your muscle strength should be developed; when in waves, you seldom stay hooked into the harness, so arms and hands should be strong and not dependent on the harness. Muscles are easily pulled in surfsailing. The body must adapt to many positions during jumping and riding waves, so flexibility is a must. Lots of stretching is recommended before any sailboarding, but in surfsailing it's crucial. One pulled muscle may mean weeks of rehabilitation, so be sure your muscles are strong and stretched before you attempt the waves.

Being aerobically fit is just as important as proper muscle tone. You never know when you may have to swim a long distance—either for your board, or if your board is gone, for the nearest beach. A wave may hold you under for an uncomfortably long period of time, and you must be physically and mentally prepared to hold your breath for that long. Without proper aerobic fitness, your life could be at stake. Even the very best surf-sailors get held under, lose their boards, and have to swim long

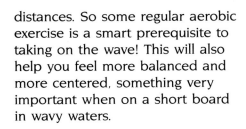

distances. So some regular aerobic exercise is a smart prerequisite to taking on the wave! This will also help you feel more balanced and more centered, something very important when on a short board in wavy waters.

HOW TO CATCH A WAVE

Catching that first wave is an all-time thrill for any sailboarder who has been "psyching up" to give it a try. For those with no prior surfing experience there can be a certain amount of mystery in the process of selecting a wave and actually initiating the ride. In fact, catching a wave on a sailboard is a surprisingly simple task.

Before sailing in the surf for the first time, take a few minutes to check conditions (see "Safety" in this chapter) and take note of where the waves are forming up and how long they roll before breaking. Your initial effort should never be in waves that are breaking hard onshore ("shorebreak"). Plan to catch the wave as far out as possible beyond the breaking area ("impact zone").

Once you've sailed from the beach all the way out beyond the

surf line (see "Getting Out Through the Surf," page 144), watch for a "set" of waves forming out at sea. Make a smooth, arc-like jibe around so that you're moving toward shore and can set-up to catch the wave of your choice. Sail on a close reach or even hard on the wind, glancing over your shoulder to synchronize with the approaching wave behind you. As the wave nears your stern, bear off slightly and you should catch it. A quick pump or two might be necessary if the wind is light or your timing is off.

Once you feel yourself catching the wave, take care to keep your weight far enough back to prevent "pearling" (driving the

board's nose under water). And take care not to take off on a wave that is excessively steep or already breaking.

The basic approach to riding a wave is to stay close to the power of the wave—the part that is breaking—and ride it as far as possible. A variety of maneuvers can be done while riding the wave which will help you to stay close to the "peak."

In onshore winds, you will want to ride the waves with your back to the wave in a close hauled position. It will be nearly impossible to ride the wave facing it since you would have to go straight downwind to stay on the wave. In offshore winds, the opposite is true, you must ride with the wind to stay on a beam reach (fastest point of sail) and you will be facing the wave. To try and ride in the opposite direction would mean sailing directly into the wind which is not possible in any sailboat. The optimum wind direction is direct side shore, which enables you to go in either direction on a wave and give you the opportunity to do a number of tricks and maneuvers.

SPECIAL EQUIPMENT NOTES

Equipment goes through stress and hard knocks when in waves—you must have confidence that it will hold together through all the tumbles. If not, you should be ready to do a lot of paddling!

Universals should be either bolted to the board or a system should be used that guarantees non-separation. If the universal pops out of your board in wave conditions, it can be next to impossible to get it back in. So be sure that this connection is very secure! Masts should be in excellent condition—well reinforced in any weak spots. Sails should be free from rips or holes, because one good tumble through a wave will make that small tear into a two-piece sail!

RIGGING CARE

Rigging procedures must be more carefully attended to in surfsailing. Take your time and double check everything. Inhaul, downhaul, and outhaul connections are critical;

they must be very secure. If a line comes undone in the middle of a multi-wave set, you'll be cursing yourself for your lack of competence in knot tying! Be sure your lines are not frayed, and take extra time in trying knots—you'll be glad you did! Before entering the water, give your rig one last check; it's well worth the few extra seconds.

SAFETY

Safety and precaution have a much bigger part in surfsailing than in any other aspect of this sport. Danger is a part of playing in waves. You're dealing with an extremely powerful force which must be treated with respect. If not handled with respect, but instead with stupidity and ignorance, unnecessary misfortune, or even tragedy may occur. So let's look at some safety techniques to keep in mind.

It's an old cliche, but quite appropriate: "Look before you leap!" Take a few minutes and sit on the beach—observe what's happening. Exactly which way is the wind blowing? Is there enough wind to get

out through the waves? Are there currents to think about? What's the best path to take out? Exactly where do I want to be? Watch the other sailors for a while, see where the problem spots are and try to avoid them.

Above all, ask yourself (and answer honestly), "are these conditions over my head?" And don't be foolish and let your ego and pride alter your decision. When in doubt, don't! If you go out in conditions that you can't handle, you're apt to break a mast, rip a sail, or ding a board. So be prepared to spend some money, that stuff no one seems to have enough of these days. And no amount of money can replace an injured body. So again, use common sense; don't be afraid to head down the coast to some smaller surf to practice.

One question often asked is "What do I do if I wipe out in the waves?" If you can't water-start and get out of there before the next wave hits, you should grab the mast tip and hold it into the waves. As the wave hits, take a deep breath and go under with it while holding onto the mast tip. If the wave is too strong, let go and after it passes start swimming toward your rig.

This is where being fit comes in. The faster you can swim and get to your board, the less beat up you and your board will be.

A few other things to keep in mind if you decide you want to challenge the waves: always look out on the horizon at what's coming. You're not only dealing with the next wave, but the entire set. if you fall on wave number one, you're going to get beaten up by wave number two, three, four, etc. So be conservative at first. Remember, one of the biggest secrets to surviving in waves is "Don't Fall!!!" Do whatever needs to be done to prevent falling. Once down, then the trouble begins! So always think ahead. Be planning a wave or two in advance; how you're going to handle that huge third wave of the set instead of only being concerned with what's right in front of you. If you don't like what you see out there, if that third wave looks a bit much, then jibe in between waves and get the heck out of there! That's why feeling confident in your jibes is a must before heading through the breakers. You sometimes must make very rapid decisions. Jibe now or take a chance at getting crunched.

Safety in the surf is of critical concern. Judgement is paramount, and skill is an absolute prerequisite. If in trouble think of your body first and your equipment second.

(Top) Gradual Bottom, Mushy Wave
(Bottom) Steep Incline, Hollow Wave

WAVES, CURRENTS AND SWELLS

Before venturing into the surf, it's important to have some understanding of the ocean and what makes a wave break. Swells are generated by offshore winds caused by storms (sometimes thousands of miles away). These swells travel until they reach shallow enough water to break. The contour of the ocean floor determines how a wave will break, depending on how deep or shallow it is and how gradual an incline the bottom has. For example, a bottom with a very gradual incline from deep to shallow will produce mushy waves that are softer breaking since they are slowed gradually by the bottom; whereas a steep bottom will produce steep and hollow waves which are more powerful and dangerous compared to soft waves. The bottom can be sand, rock or coral reef and you should know what it is before venturing out. Coral is the most dangerous because it is sharp and can cut easily and cause infections. Sand bottoms are best for first time surfsailing.

Once you're familiar with the bottom, learn to know the currents so that if you should get separated from your board, you'll know which way to swim. The next and most important consideration is wind strength and direction. This should determine which size sail and board you should use to avoid sinking or being overpowered. The direction of the wind in the surge will determine which way you can or cannot ride and jump waves. Generally, the wind will be blowing onshore, sideshore or offshore.

GETTING OUT THROUGH THE SURF

To get out through the surf, you must learn how to pop over waves without losing too much speed. In sideshore conditions, it's not as difficult because you are already heading straight out which is the proper way to approach a wave or whitewater—dead on. In onshore conditions, because you will be traveling out at a 45-degree angle to the surf, you must head your board straight into the wave and pop your board over the wave, letting the whitewater rush under the nose of your board just before you hit the wave. It is important to maintain speed by staying on a beam reach until the last possible second, then head straight up the wave and immediately bear away and regain speed before the next wave comes. All of this will take a bit of practice, but with perserverance you will be enjoying the art of surfsailing with many other enthusiasts.

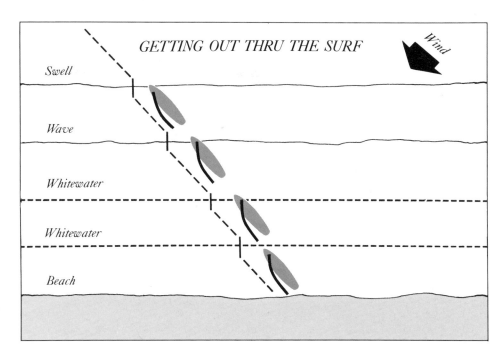

GETTING OUT THRU THE SURF

Wind

Swell

Wave

Whitewater

Whitewater

Beach

WAVE JUMPING

One of the greatest feelings on a performance sailboard is getting airborne. And, it is not as difficult as it sounds. Just applying maximum speed to a nice bump in the water will launch you. The first consideration in jumping a swell, wave or chop is to maintain maximum speed. This is true particularly in chop jumping since the waves are blowing in the same direction as the wind.

In order to get the most air possible, you want to go as fast as you can, straight up the swell. With chop or onshore winds, you cannot go straight up the wave or straight into the wind. For this reason, when jumping chop you must maintain full speed on a beam reach and be alert for a nice piece of chop that will be coming at a side angle into your board. The larger the chop, the higher you'll go relative to your speed. Try to coordinate a strong gust of wind with a nice swell, wave, or chop and use your speed to hit the ramp you've picked out. Just as the nose of your board is about to go up the ramp, head up slightly with the nose of your board so that you are heading more up the face or steep part of the

wave but not so much so that you lose speed by pointing too high into the wind. It is important, at this time, to maintain the proper sheet tension on your sail. Too often people tend to sheet out or release the power slightly as their board is about to leave the water. What you should do is sheet in and squeeze the sail toward you, then tuck your knees in and lift the board as you leave the water. The positioning of your sail and board are what give you control in the air.

When jumping waves in sideshore winds, since you are already going straight up the face on a beam reach, it is not necessary to head the board up into the wind. You can hit the wave straight on at maximum speed; and really fly high!

Wave jumping can be practiced in small surf and white water; learning takes some time. Those who tackle the big surf have years of experience and hundreds of hours of practice.

9 DESIGN REVOLUTION

S ailboard design and experimentation has been in continuous development since the inception of the original Windsurfer. This chapter, though tracing the colorful pace of revolutionary breakthrough in board development over time, reveals a smooth and sensible evolutionary thread that seems both artful and scientific. Boardsailing is a sport practiced by the passionate, formed by artists, made feasible by innovators and engineers, and pushed forth by businessmen.

Join us with nautical journalist Bruce C. Brown in a fascinating look at an evolution formed from many isolated "revolutions."

THE BAJA BOARD

Before Hoyle Schweitzer finalized the design of the original Windsurfer, he and co-designer Jim Drake went through a plethora of design approaches. The working name for their youthful design child was "Baja Board." There were numerous variations on this, their first sailboard.

Hand shaping from tandem sized polyurethane foam surfboard blanks, Schweitzer and Drake built long Baja Boards, short Baja Boards, wide Baja Boards, narrow Baja Boards —a seemingly endless combination of shapes and sizes. Their shaping ideas came from

the same place as their materials, surfing. Unlike the Europeans who began building boards in the mid 1970's, the southern Californians' roots were in surfing—not yachting—and their early Baja Boards reflected this.

THE ORIGINAL WINDSURFER

The "Windsurfer," a balanced offspring of myriad Baja Boards, is a more complex design than the casual glance would indicate. Most sailors tend to think the bottom of the board is flat, but careful examination of the original "plug" for the board reveals that not a single inch of the surface is flat. The entire surface consists of well-thought-out curvatures. Clearly, the original Windsurfer was a compromise. Shape and mass were designed for maneuverability, stability, and flotation. The rails were designed "soft," (rounded as opposed to sharply tapered or egg-like) for maneuverability.

There were very real manufacturing considerations taken into account. With roto-molding construction a tangible possibility, design factors had to be kept feasible from a practical point of view. The mast step, and to a lesser degree the skeg box, were designed to conform to the roto-molding capacities of the time. These and also the daggerboard trunk are studies in design simplicity. The Windsurfer was in fact the first production sailboard to be roto-molded with a "through-hull" (hole all the way through for the mast step and daggerboard).

THE REVOLUTION BEGINS

Unlike many compromises, the Windsurfer worked! People began to Windsurf! Naturally, competition among sailors ensued; as soon as people learned to boardsail they wanted to see who was best and fastest. The new toys were introduced to course racing and ocean waves. Soon human experimentation and ever-increasing ability stretched and finally outstripped the design parameters of the boards. Working in backyard shops in California and Hawaii, home board shapers tried their own innovations. Many of these did not work, but some were effective, and the design revolution found fuel. Shapes, sizes, rail contours, daggerboards, and skegs were changed and changed again. Footstraps were established, enabling sailors to stay solid and steady on their boards through gusty wind, choppy waters, and while in the air after launching through waves.

A SPORT IS BORN

Far Left: Surfing and "windsurfing;"
(ancestor meets newborn.)
Left: Original production Windsurfer
is strikingly similar to modern versions.
Top: Experimentation in sailboard design
commenced as sailors' feats required more
specialized hardware.

THE PERFORMANCE IMPERATIVE

While design evolution in Europe was tending toward "yachty" displacement-type (rounded bottom) boards, in America the focus was on "fun" boards. To many, especially the southern Californians and Hawaiians, "fun" meant ocean waves. By 1980 a number of custom board builders were turning out their own versions of high performance boards, based upon requirements necessary for successful wave riding. These boards varied greatly in design, engineering, and effectiveness; some were advancements, others throw-aways. If a design worked, it became a new starting point for still further development as builders and sailors leapfrogged to higher performance levels. If a board was a failure, the ideas tried were proven as impractical and as such sped progress by showing designers what not to do.

Coastal waters became the performance lab for creative experiments that were to affect boards of all kinds worldwide. Two things that early experimental boards had in common were length and thickness. Roughly, boards were in the 10-foot range. They were all "up-haulers," so for flotation they were thick, many having large concentrations of foam in the tail. To keep the weight of these long, thick boards manageable, most builders turned to super lightweight foam blanks and high-tech Kevlar for their skins.

This era also saw many experiments with underwater foils—the skegs and daggerboards. Some builders tried replacing daggerboards and their attendant slots with skegs mounted in fin boxes. The large area of a daggerboard is shaped as an efficient hydrodynamic foil to give lift; a skeg is slab-side designed for tracking stability. The outcome of this particular experiment was questionable, but led some builders to discard daggerboards entirely and focus on fin groupings at the tail.

THE SURFBOARD INFLUENCE

Two important and unconnected occurrences took place in the early era of sailboard progressive design. The first was the "water start." Developed as a maneuver in a freestyle routine, the water start opened the door to "sinker" boards. Shapers were finally free to design boards that did not have to support the sailor's weight while at rest.

A second occurrence was the increased involvement of surfboard designers in the making of sailboards. Here, custom wave board building took a quantum leap forward. Surfboard builders brought not only their board-making mastery to sailboarding—but also their advanced knowledge of what was effective in ocean waves. It seems easier for the experienced surfboard shapers to learn to deal with the dynamics of the sailing rig than for sail-oriented designers to learn the effects of waves on boards. Possibly this is because once into a wave a board is no longer sailing—it is *surfing*.

SURFING AND SAILING

no longer just "sailboards." At length, surfsailing competitions spawned a compromise which brought about boards effective for wave riding, wave jumping, and also flat water sailing.

Contest judging and the advent of "ins-and-outs" style racing placed a premium on maneuverability, thus designers began producing "all around" wave boards. Such boards formed the backbone from which performance standards could develop.

The intensified rush to produce perfect solutions to performance

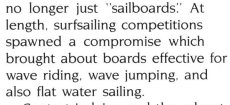

Wave sailing found its capitol in Hawaii. With year-round sun, tradewinds, and waves, the Hawaiian environment sent sailboard development into warp speed. Island shapers were able to translate design theory into working models and have them in the water almost immediately. A sketch drawn in clean Hawaiian sand on Monday could be ready to sail by Friday,

and in Hawaii there was no wait for the right conditions for a test ride. Somewhere there were wind and waves. In many cases the hot board in March was out-designed in May.

During this period of rapid advancement, the format of wave sailing contests and the criterion of judging skill was being formed, altered, and formed again. Sailboard surfing and wave jumping became a sub-sport—a specialty that asked questions about all board and rig theory and one that bred skills of a new and spectacular kind. Riders sailed fast and furious on flat water, jumped high into the air over waves enroute to open ocean, then pivoted and caught rolling swells that crested into wild waves. There were "jumping" boards, and pure "wave riding" boards,

Early experiments with sailboards for surfsailing fueled a "design revolution" in sailboards and components which has affected all facets of boardsailing.

Sailboard "foil" design—skegs and daggerboards—has spanned wide spectrums, from the necessary to the nutty. Today's sailboard owners are the benefactors of many experiments, some successful and many mistaken.

  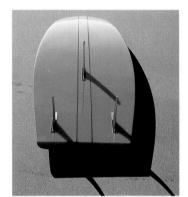

SPEED & FLIGHT

imperatives came to need a cooling. Gradually, the giddy era of monthly "break-through" designs began to slow and evolve into a period of refinement of basic proven board types. At this writing there is still no perfect compromise between wave riders, wave jumpers, and flat water sailboards. But wonderful solutions have been achieved that emphasize one maneuver and offer plausible ability to apply other maneuvers.

At the forefront of sailboard performance since youth, sailor/ designer Mike Waltze and his Sail-

boards Maui company have consistently produced advancements in sailboards over time. In 1983, a Waltze designed board piloted by expert Fred Haywood smashed the world sailboard speed record with a 35.49 mph top speed.

Waltze's boards have been used by multiple contest winners and Mike Waltze himself has been regarded by many as the best and most versatile performance board-sailor in the world. Operating on the proving ground of Maui's north shore, Waltze refines his designs year-round in a locale with ideal conditions and weather variances for high demand boardsailing.

WAVE JUMPING SPECIALIZATION

Boards designed by Waltze with an emphasis on wave jumping are slightly longer, wider, and have

more flotation than their wave riding sisters. These "sinkers" only begin to exercise their potential in 12 to 15-knots of wind. Sailors of average size ride jump boards measuring around 8 ft. 10-inches which weigh an average of twenty pounds. Their maximum beam is about 24 inches; tail width is over 16 inches. (Following surfing tradition, both nose and tail dimensions are taken at a foot from either end of the board).

The secret of the jumper's performance is in its tail. The board carries its maximum beam well aft and ends in an abruptly squared-off tail. With its flat bottom and added flotation, the jump board can accelerate quickly, an important factor for judgement positioning among fast rolling shoreward swells. The wide tail also keeps the board planing all the way up the face of the wave, giving that last little kick to the jump. Under the tail is typically a tri-fin arrangement, with a single large fin farthest aft and two smaller "thruster" fins farther forward and outboard. Located in fin boxes, the fin system can be tuned to meet conditions either by changing position, size, or the number of fins used. To enable the sailor to shift body weight, there are often two pairs of footstraps forward and two straps in line on the tail.

WAVE RIDING SPECIALIZATION

A "pure" wave *riding* board is generally smaller than a jump board. A sailor using an 8'10" jump board would use roughly an 8-foot wave rider. The shorter, narrower, thinner board would weigh just 12 pounds. Aside from the smaller size of the wave rider, the noticeable difference in the two is the narrow, drawn-out "pintail" aft section of the wave board. As in surfboards, the

pintail also features more "rocker" than the wide tail jump board. Only a single fin is needed to keep the narrow pintail on track, though fin size and location are still alterable to meet conditions.

In wave jumping the narrow pintail design does not plane up the face of a wave as well as the wide square tail of the jump board. It also loses power as it punches through the crest of the wave, rather than lifting off. Wave board decks are usually slightly cleaner in appearance, usually featuring only a single set of footstraps forward and two straps in line aft. On the ultra-short boards, a rider needs only to move the rear foot a few inches and shift weight slightly to effect dramatic changes in direction.

CREATIVE COMPROMISE

One popular attempt to combine the best features of both wave jumping and wave riding boards is the "winger" pintail design. Winger-type boards, at this writing, tend to be full in the forward section. And, as in the basic jump board configuration, aft sections are fairly beamy. But then something happens. In the aft quarter the winger sprouts mini sculptured wing nubs.

These "wings" cause a sharp change of format which fashions into a pintail at the rear and incorporates a unique tri-fin arrangement for steady tracking capability. The larger fin is aft, under the tip of the tail, and the smaller "thruster" fins are somewhat forward under the wings. Although rideable in certain conditions without the thrusters, placement of the wings and thrusters are critical with the winger and can produce either a superbly dynamic performer or an unrideable monstrosity. Definitely a game for experts.

SAILBOARD ENGINEERING FACTORS

With board construction and componentry unraveling new chapters continuously, development seems non-stop. However some interesting principles prevail. After much experimentation, Waltze boards have adopted an efficient and simple mast base constructed from a single fin box! From the basic mast base slot of the original Windsurfers, designers strayed far in the methods of attaching rigs to boards. One of the many systems that evolved was the use of a pair of fin boxes mounted parallel and on either side of the center stringer. The mast was then mounted on a stainless steel mast step with twin slides riding in the fin boxes. This system was adjustable and strong enough to take high stress loads, but it was clumsy, complicated, heavy, and expensive. A later alternative was a single fin box positioned in between two parallel center stringers. Thusly, the two strips of wood that provide internal longitudinal strength and stiffness to the board do double duty by taking the lateral loading of the rig.

Experimentation with exotic outer skins has extended into materials such as Kevlar® for high strength/low weight objectives. However, fiberglass remains the dominant skin due to versatility, availability, cost, and workability. And due to the shortness of modern

ENTER: TECHNOLOGY

BOLD IDEAS

wave and jump boards, the modicum of reduced weight from Kevlar has thus far proven marginal. Further, where Kevlar was initially utilized in an effort to reduce board breakages in heavy surf conditions, such breakages are much less frequent today due to reduced board lengths and quality resins and fiberglass available to builders. Not to mention that the very shortness of state-of-the-art surf purpose sailboards now means less total skin weight than when such boards were longer. Waltze boards, for example, are typically skinned with a layer of 6 ounce and a layer of 4 ounce "S-glass" on the bottom, and layers of 6, 6, and 4 ounce on the deck area. Extra reinforcement is added at the mast step, footstraps, tail, and fin boxes. It has been learned that multi-layers (such as 4 ounce over 6 ounce) is stronger than a single layer of 10 ounce fiberglass. The resin is applied "hot" (high catalyst to resin ratio) so that it gels and hardens in minimal working time. This prevents resin from being soaked up by the foam of the blank, resulting in a lighter, stronger skin.

THE ASYMMETRICAL DEPARTURE

To those who experiment with sailboard shapes, even the eye-pleasing symmetry of design is not sacred. Asymmetry, like so much else in wave sailing, has its roots in surfing. In surfing, asymmetry evolved from the knowledge that turns off the bottom of waves placed different demands on a board than "cut-back" turns off the tops of waves. As such, two sides of the board were being required to perform different tasks. Obviously, an asymmetrically shaped board would be effective in one direction only, well suited for surfing locations where waves break or "peel" in one predominant direction.

Asymmetrical sailboards can be recognized by their outline contour, wherein one side of the board is shaped differently than the other—essentially toward the tail. In effect, the asymmetrical sailboard combines two tails on one board. Specifically for the skilled wave riding boardsailor, the asymmetrical design is effective for surfsailing in which a narrow board and tail are desirable for fast "bottom turns," yet a wider board and tail are desired for "cutback" maneuvers. A "best of both worlds" theory.

THE "FUNBOARD" CONCEPT

Closely following the development of short board design for wave riding, wave jumping, and high speed performance, the "funboard" concept was born.

Whereas short boards were the tools with which to make real the outer-most dreams of speed and wave performance, funboards have brought performance thrills to the common boardsailor. High tech specialized boards require highly developed specialized skills. Without those skills a rider finds frustration and trouble. The funboard concept makes performance accessible to sailors with moderate skills.

In size, modern funboards are usually shorter than stock recreational boards, yet considerably larger than the largest category of "short" boards. The design range of these boards is so great that it's nearly impossible to describe a "typical" funboard, however most have fundamentals in common. At this writing 95% of the major sailboard producers offer one or more funboard models in their product line.

Most funboards can be uphauled, although some do in fact classify as sinkers and as such require that their rider know how to water start. Funboard shapes are as different as their lengths; a single manufacturer's line might feature a winger swallow tail funboard, a rounded pintail, a square tail funboard, and a winger pintail! Their underwater foils are equally varied, ranging from tri-fin clusters without a daggerboard to single fins with fully retractable or kick-up daggerboard.

FUNBOARD FUN

The uses of funboards are a matter of imagination. Their hallmark is versatility and their characteristic is performance. Shorter funboards can be used in waves, while longer funboards find their niche in power sailing on lakes, bays, beach, and ocean stretches. Like sports cars, they carve smooth radical turns, accelerate quickly, and sustain high speeds with stability. Funboards are a design step above stock sailboards, offering a buyer the ability to select a model that's best suited to his personal sailing style, desired use and local sailing conditions.

FUNBOARD SPECIALIZATION

While many board builders were making boards shorter for fun in the waves, there were those who found their enjoyment in high-speed power reaching on flat water. These were folks who liked to plant

their feet in footstraps, hoist their daggerboards and go fast!

Funboard development in areas other than wave riding applications began with "Pan Am boards." These were boards designed to compete in the prestigious Pan Am World Cup, a unique event held annually by the Kailua Bay Windsurfing Association and originally sponsored by Pan American Airlines. Staged in Hawaii's Kailua Bay on the island of Oahu, the rigors of this event necessitate that a board perform in several ways. Unlike a wave board which changes direction by jibing and maneuvers with snap responsiveness under power assistance from both wave and wind, a Pan Am board must go to weather, reach, run, and sustain prolonged speed over lengthy stretches. A Pan Am board must have the stability and planing characteristics necessary to spend long periods of time on a single, fast moving ground swell. And yet this board must also be able to negotiate the surf!

Early on, the production model "Windsurfer Rocket 12" was an ideal competitive funboard for the Pan Am competitor. However as in all competitive arenas, when racing became keener and more lucrative, board refinement intensified. Pan Am "funboards" became Pan Am "experimental" boards. And while they veered off into their own departure, funboard design and technology continued to benefit.

PAN AM BOARD STATE-OF-THE-ART

At this writing, World Cup boards (formerly "Pan Am") continue to impact funboard design. Although comparison of a "real live" World Cup board to almost any production funboard reveals differences, both share precepts in common.

World Cup, (Pan Am) boards are instantly recognized by their length—some exceeding 13-feet. Widths seem proportionally narrow. Earlier designs were often four to six inches thick, employing squarish "boxy" rails. Boards weighing in

Top: Hi-tech Kevlar has been one of a handful of super-lightweight skinnings used in the construction of experimental wave boards and especially World Cup funboards.
Above: "Asymmetrical" configuration is one of many fascinating experiments in the evolution of sailboards for surfsailing use.
Right: Production high performance funboards (inset) share increasing similarities with full race World Cup equipment (bottom).

WORLD CUP RACING

excess of 35 pounds have now trimmed several pounds in many cases. Sharply pointed noses with once as much as a foot of "rocker" now exhibit slightly less—roughly eight inches. Rocker extends gradually sternward to approximately five feet from the nose tip. From the mid section back, classic World Cup boards have either flat-bottom planing surfaces or are slightly V'd.

A period of wide, boxy tails with twin fins lasted for a time; these tail designs provided great speed but made boards difficult to jibe and incurred drag when going to weather. Tail sections have evolved to general widths of twelve to thirteen inches, drawing into narrow squared or rounded pintails. Experimental development will continue to focus here.

The underside of a "conventional" world cup board is a study in "clean" design. A single high aspect ratio skeg is mounted aft for directional stability. The high aspect ratio centerboard, or "blade," designed for maximum lift at speed when going to weather, can be completely retracted. The "door" where the blade is retracted is closed by either a rubber, plastic, or dacron gasket when the blade is in the up position. This enables an unobstructed planing surface.

A "concave" underside has been experimented with periodically, with some significant success and a few drawbacks. Like so many other sail-

boarding breakthroughs, the concept of concave hulls is not a new idea—however execution of the concept is the key to performance.

Concave hulls have been seen on racing power boats and surfboards for years. The theory behind the design is simple: double longitudinal hollows are carved out on either side of the central stringers; the water moves faster through these hollows than it would across the surface of the hull. The hollows also provide for less wetted surface so the boards accelerate faster.

In World Cup races where boards with double concave hulls have competed against conventional World Cup, most sailors have conceded that the concaves were as much as twenty percent faster and also pointed higher to windward. Further, sailor Fred Haywood incorporated the double concave design into his renown Sailboards Maui speed board. With this board he set the world speed record for sailboards at 30.82 knots (35.49 mph) at Weymouth England in October 1983.

Interestingly, concaves have found their way into the production market place. At this writing several manufacturers are offering high performance double concave designs.

A competitive World Cup sailor will carry a quiver of blades to balance against the forces of the rig he has chosen for a given set of weather conditions. If he has gone with a large sail he will need a deep blade, while a small sail requires a shallower blade.

The deck of a World Cup board is a busy place. To shift weight, a sailor needs three or four sets of footstraps near the centerboard and three straps in line at the narrow tail. Between the forward footstraps is the top of the blade. Like a gearshift, the sailor kicks the blade handle

forward to retract the centerboard into the slot for minimum drag and maximum speed. Farther forward there is an adjustable mast track. The mast step is locked in position by the track until the sailor releases it with his foot. Then he can push the mast base forward when going to weather, or pull it aft while on a reach when reduced wetted surface is desirable. The board's twin stringers sandwich the fin box, daggerboard cavity, and sliding mast track, easing the lateral stress loading on the rig and foils.

The length and mass of an average Pan Am board makes the search for weight reduction significant. Many of the hottest versions are skinned with carbon fiber/Kevlar laminates used in combination with both "S" and "K-glass" for strength and lightness. Core materials receive the same attention. The well known Clark polyurethane ultra-lite foam blank has given way to experiments with even lighter styrofoam construction. Clearly, these technologies apply to the racer reaching for advantage over a competitor that may measure only seconds in a one hour race. Most production boards do not incorporate such esoteric materials and don't need to.

Like the wave sailing and wave jumping boards earlier described, modern World Cup style boards are undergoing continuous experimentation and development. These are the test-lab arenas for boardsailing. However, after a decade of research and development extremes, the 80's decade hints at a refinement period in design parameters, materials, and componentry.

FOIL DESIGN

While the "try-it-and-see-if-it-works" period of sailboard design seems to have shifted from spotlight to twilight, innovation continues in pockets of focus. Among these, skeg design is paramount. The riddles yet to be solved are questions of number, placement, shape and the long-time problem of cavitation.

With state-of-the-art surfboards

sprouting clusters of four, and even five fins, this proliferation has found its way to sailboards. Location of fins, even with the built-in adjustability provided by fin boxes, is always being tested with single, twin, and tri-fin boards. And fin shape variations seem to be endless.

The problem of fin cavitation has been approached in a variety of ways, ever since this phenomenon was isolated. The uniquely shaped "football fin," and also ribbed or "fence fin" appear viable but imperfect solutions.

STATE-OF-THE-ART FOR THE CONSUMER

With the '80's has come production sophistication that offers design flexibility and real quality. Today, the sailor desiring a high performance board can go to his local sailboard shop and select from a multitude of up-to-the-minute production boards. Once made, the investment in a reputable high performance board is a good one, incorporating durability, resale value, and purpose.

While the impressive new production boards have much to offer, custom boards still offer some very real advantages. They are fractionally stiffer and lighter than most production boards and can be built precisely the way a sailor wants. Durability is inferior, but the "personal touch" of an expert hand

craftsman offers timeless appeal.

Sophisticated boardsailing consumers are seeing a revolution before their eyes in quality and variety of sailboards, both custom and production built. This is a sign of a healthy infant sport getting the nourishment it needs.

MODERN COMPONENTRY

*A*long arduous day of racing is behind you as you sail back to the beach. Nearing the shore under a setting sun you feel fatigued but strangely unsettled... if only there would be one more race; "I could win it, I could win it.!"

This is what racing is all about; not winning, per se, but the *will* to win. Racing is a test of maximum individual effort, an effort that comes from energy, desire, and positive mental discipline. For the business executive, computer programmer, sales person, professor, carpenter, and student alike, sailboard racing is the great equalizer—an arena fueled by the willingness to try and try again, regardless of age, creed, or station. On the race course, your competitor's drive to do his best is matched only by yours; mutual respect transcends all barriers.

Gaining the knowledge and skills necessary to win a sailboard race is often a lengthy process. The shortest route to winning is personal improvement, and personal improvement is, of course, achieved through systematic perseverance. Not dogged persevervance—but a consistent striving, utilizing a system of self measuring and self improvement.

HARDWARE

Make sure your equipment is competitive. A few scratches on the board or a small wrinkle in your sail shouldn't be enough to spell defeat. Great sailors can go out on "junk" equipment and win. But this is no reason to bypass every reasonable attempt to keep equipment in top condition. This may include wet sanding (600 grit) your hull and daggerboard for optimum smoothness and rolling the sail on a cardboard tube to minimize creases. Be sure to transport all components with great care, keeping them protected and away from excessive sunlight or heat. Just knowing that your equipment is in top shape can often make the difference in confidence necessary to help your psychological edge, in addition to your equipment boost.

PHYSICAL PREPARATION

There is no greater physical exercise for racing than sailing itself. True boardsailing fanatics become almost obsessive about sailing. They feel that if they don't practice, some other competitor will—and maybe gain an edge. It isn't necessary to take racing this seriously, but top competitors often do.

When practicing for racing, the most important factors that need concentration are physical stamina and board maneuverability. For developing stamina, sailing on long tacks without a harness is the best method. Some really gung-ho competitors go out "pumping" instead of simply sailing. Other sailors lower their inhaul (boom attachment position) in order to get less leverage from the rig, necessitating more arm strength. When it's all said and done, a good indicator of having practiced hard enough is when you come in from a sail and the calouses on your hands sting.

DEVELOPING SPEED

With determination and luck, it's possible to finish near the leaders once in a while, but in order to win you've got to be legitimately fast. Unfortunately, sailing on reaches all day long on a high performance short board won't develop well rounded racing skills. To be fast around a triangle course you've got to be practiced on a regatta board and adept at sailing each racing "leg."

Top Left: silent, careful preparation.
Middle Left: speed, the name of the game.
This Photo: the buddy system; two boat
practicing sharpens skills.
Right: "kangaroo stance" has proved universally
effective for upwind sailing.

The triangle course puts special emphasis on four different points of sail; beating, reaching, broad reaching, and running. It also puts emphasis on maneuvers such as sailing stationary (at the start), tacking and mark roundings (windward, reaching, and leeward). All of these techniques should be practiced until they become second nature.

To learn these maneuvers and to learn how to deal with the subtle nuances of triangle racing, it's best to makeshift your own triangle practice course. In most places boardsailors sail, there are anchored boats, channel markers, or lobster pots that can be used to set up a "course." If none of these exist, then a few empty plastic jugs and a hundred feet of clothesline (for anchoring the marks) will do the trick.

On this course, practice every maneuver that comes into play during the course of a real race. Try to envision an imaginary ghost racer to race against. A second saved by an efficiently completed tack or jibe is progress. Strive for this. By minimizing the time taken by maneuvers and by maximizing speed on the course overall, your knowledge and skill can soon surpass 75% of your competitors.

TWO BOAT PRACTICING

The benefit of two sailors working together to improve performance is clearly superior to practicing alone. Since most races are won and lost on the windward leg, practice should focus heavily on sailing to weather.

Without another board as a measure, it's often very difficult to remember to point competitively close to the wind. By having a comparable sailor directly in view to leeward and slightly ahead (safe leeward position), a windward sailor has something tangible to gauge position and speed by. Find a friend who wants to get better, then go sailing and exchange safe leeward position. Each time one of you gets too far ahead, slow down and get back in position again. This technique for self improvement is not only efficient but it's also fun. It brings out the best in both of you. Significant improvement is the inevitable result.

SAILING UPWIND

Through trial and error over time, several sailing techniques or stances have proved fast. To achieve good performance upwind, the sail's force must be directed via body geometry directly through the center of lateral resistance (daggerboard). The popular "kangaroo" stance (see photo), developed in the mid 1970's, is still the most universally applied method of achieving this.

A second upwind fundamental

is the ability to "point" very close to the wind. To practice this, head the board gradually closer and closer to the wind while sailing on a beat. Concentrate on the feel of the water flowing across the daggerboard. As the daggerboard gradually stalls, forward speed decreases and the board begins to slip sideways. Somewhere between sailing for speed and pointing too close to the wind you begin "pinching." Pinching is not always a fast way to sail, but it can be very useful in different racing situations. Whether trying to squeak past a mark or working out from underneath a competitor after a start, pinching is a useful and necessary skill to master.

REACHING

This is a point of sail that rewards good sailing with the greatest gains over a specific distance sailed. Reaching should be practiced in a wide variety of conditions, as techniques for achieving maximum speed vary with wind and water variances. Sometimes its faster to stand with hands and feet far apart, while other times it's faster to sail in the kangaroo position. A good guideline to follow is to maintain a little extra pull on the back sailing hand and to place your feet in much the same position as in footstraps on funboards (or in the footstraps if it's a funboard race).

Pumping (using the sail like a wind paddle) when reaching is a widely used technique, even though it's strictly outlawed in standard One Design racing rules. But to win you've got to know all the tricks, so its mandatory to perfect your pumping, as with all other skills. In international competition (where pumping is most flagrant) expert pumping is necessary, unless you want to be passed by fifty racers on one leg of the course!

BROAD REACHING AND RUNNING

Sailing downwind, either through broad reaching or running dead downwind, requires special attention to sail trim and weight placement. A cardinal mistake is to stand too far back on the board; this sinks the stern and makes you go slow.

In swells or chop, broad reaching takes on a new dimension. Most sailors find themselves riding a surface swell until it dissipates. At this time the board kind of wallows in the backwash, waiting for the next swell to follow. It is possible, however, to ride one wave onto another, minimizing lost time. Swells are like bricks on the water's surface. To jump from one "brick" to another, do as follows: ride a swell until it just starts to decline, then cut either left or right to catch the next wave (which usually follows closely aside). Don't think that all this extra distance sailed is slower. The distance gained from a wave far outmeasures a little juggling to speed forward motion. A straight line downwind is definitely not always the fastest route to take; often a zig-zag is faster.

THE REGATTA SITE

Competitors often talk about local knowledge playing a big part in racing success. This is valid to some

Rewards can be reaped on race course reaching legs.

extent, but with a little research you can all but nullify this rule.

Strategy is a plan for efficient execution of skills and knowledge. Researching the particular subtleties of a regatta site can and should be done even before ever sailing in the area. The first thing to do when researching a race site is to get a chart of the area from a ship's chandlery or the nearest Coast Guard office. Then visit or call a boardsailing store in the area and ask about what kind of conditions are expected at regatta time. Most areas either have prevailing winds or sea breezes, so sit down and actually draw these winds on your chart. Land mass directly affects wind flow, so theorize how the land will affect the wind. Diagramming the wind on a chart is almost like being able to go up in a helicopter over the race site. If you could see the wind, you would see visually how the land affects its flow. The net result for you is knowledge that can be applied while racing on the course.

Also research water depth. Ask the local sailboard dealer how much tide velocity exists at the race location; notate this on your chart. Bottom contour affects tidal direction and rate of flow. If the tidal direction opposes wind direction, surface waves become very steep and confused. Inside information such as this helps you prepare for the practical realities specific to the regatta upcoming.

After setting up on race day morning, sail out to the race course early, into the vicinity of the windward mark. Then point your board straight downwind and let the sail hang forward, flapping freely like a flag. Observe and feel the nuances of the wind's velocity and direction, imprinting them in your mind. After having drifted down near the starting line, try a practice start and sail the windward leg. Having sensed and absorbed the characteristics of where you're sailing, moment-to-moment decisions will be educated instead of random.

THE TACTICAL EDGE

Whereas strategy is the plan, tactics are the methods of carrying out the race plan. Sailboard racing is the most tactically spontaneous form of sailboat racing. The difference in distance between sailing a collision-free course and colliding with a competitor is often measured in inches, rather than feet. Racing in a big fleet is like being a New York City cab driver in rush hour. Reactions must be quick and without hesitation, enabling you to steer clear of a shaky sailor or impending collision.

THE START

An ideal starting tactic for a beginning or intermediate skipper is the "late weather end approach." Here, a sailor who is unsure about his speed or boat handling can stay safely away from close quarter maneuvering. By waiting for the boards at the windward end to clear out, a trouble-free start can be accomplished. To do this, tack onto port tack as soon as clear air is attainable. This clear air can usually be found to windward of the fleet right after the start.

Note "mid-line sag" in this classic starting line-up.

For the experienced racer, starting tactics are more numerous and varied. Many top sailors wait for the fleet to "set up" on the line, all the while holding slightly back and stalking for an opening. By approaching to windward or leeward of the line it is possible to sail into a gap in the procession and be speedily off with clear air at the gun. Still other racers prefer to approach the line on a port tack. This approach offers the best view of the "pre-start flow" and is a most opportunistic method.

Whatever the chosen approach, racing to win means getting a good

start. Timing should be within two or three seconds of the start gun, board going full speed ahead. It is highly desirable to have no one to leeward; meantime, strive to keep up with the boards to windward even if you think there is a pack of premature starters. If a pack of premature starters causes a general recall, then you are at no disadvantage. If not, you're off and away, fair and square.

An important phenomenon is "mid-line sag." In the middle of the

starting line there is commonly a collective reaction among sailors to hold back from the line a board length or two. This is due to fundamental difficulty in accurately gauging board position without a nearby buoy to sight on. If you find yourself starting in the middle of the line you can usually sheet in for speed a little earlier than the boards around you and still not be over the line early. If you are not over early once in a while, chances are you're not trying your hardest.

THE BEAT

If wind is shifty, a start that allows tacking freely is important. The two most vital factors to sailing a strong weather leg are clear air and the ability to tack on windshifts. Tacking on every single windshift isn't generally efficient or effective, but strategic tacking on major windshifts can keep you accelerating in clear air.

With magazines and books printing mountains of information pertaining to upwind racing tactics, absorbing and applying all this can be confusing. The most important rule to follow is: stay close to the majority of your best competitors and operate from this plan. Sailing far off from the core of the fleet is a gamble which may pay off once in awhile but more often ends in disaster. Your gambles should be careful and calculated.

WINDWARD MARK APPROACH

There are two basic ways of approaching the windward mark. Most racers do so on the starboard tack layline; a fleet of sailors on top 25% of the fleet, approach on port tack. And if you're back in the pack, simply do whatever is necessary to approach the mark in clear air. Even if you must over-stand the starboard layline to ensure clear air, do so. It's amazing how many boards you can pass by reaching into the mark with good speed while the boards to leeward slop around in confused wind and water.

THE REACHING LEGS

Again, clear air is of primary importance. If there are just a few competitors threatening from behind, sail high to let them know it

Top Left : split second timing enables a daring sailor to "port tack the fleet," gaining a headstart to the weather mark and clear air as he crosses the line with the gun.
Middle Left: The beat to the weather mark is often tight and congested. Fight for clean air and try to stay close to the front runners. If you're back in the pack, tack on a windshift and find unobstructed air.
Below: The weather mark can be approached from port tack or starboard; starboard is usually favored and has the right of way.

this line brings with it a confused wind. Approaching the weather mark on port tack can minimize the time sailed in "bad air." The port tack approach is great unless you are back in the pack; in this situation all the boats that have rounded the mark before you will be reaching across your otherwise clear air.

As a general rule, if you're up with the leaders, approach the weather mark on the favored (usually starboard) tack. If you're in the won't be easy to pass you. If there is a heap of boards close behind you, think fast; it might be faster to sail off to leeward of their wind-shaddows and let the masses fight it out while you sail unencumbered to the next mark.

The general rule for the reaches is to fight it out for clear air until it's not worth fighting anymore. Often times it's just good sense to let a faster sailor by, thus giving away only one place instead of fighting it out and losing five places.

REACHING MARK ROUNDING

Many positions are won or lost during the reaching mark approach and rounding. By keeping in mind how to turn the board most efficiently, try to plan your approach and rounding to make the best use of your board handling skills. During mark roundings the old adage reigns true: "better safe than sorry." Even if a sailor has every rule in the book on his side, a collision usually will result in many lost places and an untimely swim. Sail clean, sail fair, and sail dry.

LEEWARD MARK ROUNDING AND THE SECOND WINDWARD LEG

The second weather leg in a race offers an opportunity to put refined strategies to further use. The most intensely tactical part of the leg, however, begins at its point of origin: the leeward mark rounding.

Make every attempt to round the mark inside of the boat ahead, even if you have to step on the tail of the board to slow down so as to get in position. Nothing is worse than a bad leeward mark rounding; not only do people pass you like crazy but it's also just plain dumb to put yourself at a disadvantage in the first place. The ability to use your feet for rail and tail control during reaching and downwind mark roundings is an important technique. Being able to turn the board like this—surfboard style—without the sail is vital because competitors behind you will often purposely "cover" your air so as to make you round the mark wide, letting them slip inside you.

As you sail up the second windward leg again, don't wander off from the core of the fleet. Play it

smart; get with the leaders and make them work to try and beat you. Putting your opponents under pressure will give you an effective mental advantage.

THE FINISH

Pick either the port or starboard end of the finish line and aim for it. If, for example, the port end of the line was favored when you started, it's a fairly safe bet that the starboard end of the line will be favored at the finish. Commit yourself to whichever end of the line you feel is the shortest distance from where you are. If there's a competitor close astern of you, lead him past the layline so that he tacks late and cannot tack for the finish until after you have executed your final tack.

If a competitor passes you astern on port tack while you're sailing upwind on a starboard tack, then tack immediately and "sit on your opponent." If the port tack sailor is allowed to sail on and then tack back to starboard, then chances are that you (now on port tack) will have to give way. Don't let this happen.

Smart tactics are reactions which come from savvy and experience. Usually you must make a mistake three or four times before the "tactical remedy" sinks in and becomes reflex. Frequent racing will sharpen your instincts.

Success in racing is the cumulative by-product of thoughtful preparation, good board speed, sensible strategies, and quick tactical thinking. And through it all, racing should be challenging and fun regardless of your level of skill. Remember what you are out on the course for: to have fun and strive for new heights of personal fulfillment. You don't have to win every race to *win at racing*.

SKILL VS. EQUIPMENT: OLYMPIC CLASS BOARDSAILING WITH SCOTT STEELE

It was July, 1984 that U.S. Olympic boardsailing representative Scott Steele uttered the words: "the Europeans are much more experienced in Olympic Class boardsailing than we Americans; if I sail well, I can place in the top eight. If the wind is on my side and I do everything right, I may do better." In August, Steele won the Olympic Silver Medal. He missed the gold by a fractional measure.

Often, it is in the nature of a repeated winner to understate his skills, mentally disciplining himself to concentrate on how he must improve instead of reveling in past accomplishments. Scott Steele is the archtype of this vintage. He speaks softly—and performs with a wallop.

With a boyhood racing background in small monohull sailboats, chiefly 420 and Laser classes,

Scott began boardsailing in 1977 in the Windsurfer One Design class. Competition minded, he (along with his two older brothers) began entering regattas almost immediately and was winning local events within a year. Driven to challenge the best, Scott soon embarked on a national sailboard racing effort, finding himself in the water amidst the likes of Robbie Naish, Mike Waltze, Greg Aguera, Rhonda Smith, and other pillars of U.S. boardsailing. Although beaten repeatedly, he nipped at the heels of the "big names" after a short initiation and studied their techniques incessantly.

AMATEUR OR PROFESSIONAL

Competing and improving steadily throughout four years of college (achieving college all-American in sailing for two successive years), Steele graduated in 1981 and began blazing a trail. After a third place finish in the 1981 Windsurfer Americans, he proceeded to win the USBSA Eastern Championship lightweight class, the 1981 Central Open Class Championships, the 1982 BUSA Nationals, 1982 USBSA Open Class Nationals, and the 1982 Molson's North American Opens. Through these and other wins, Scott defeated competitors of top-most caliber (Naish, Waltze, and others) and was selected as a member of the U.S. Boardsailing Team. "The prospect of a good living as a professional boardsailor was available," Scott reports, but boardsailing had been accepted as an Olympic sport and he considered this a once-in-a-lifetime opportunity.

After two highly dedicated years of Olympic preparation which began with an 8th place in the 1982 Windglider Worlds in Italy, Scott earned a down-to-the-wire spot as the U.S.A.'s boardsailing representative in the final Olympic Trials of June, 1984. The British "Windglider" was the specified board type, a European One Design brand.

MAN OR MACHINE

"Everyone competing on the same board and rig is the purest way to measure skill," Scott emphasises. He notes that much of modern sailboard racing is very "equipment sensitive," citing the well known World Funboard Cup as a series in which hi-tech equipment can have a substantial bearing on the outcome of races. "The Windglider is a board that makes every competitor work equally hard," says Steele. The board is large and buoyant enough to offer heavier sailors sufficient advantage against lightweights in light air conditions, while its ample 71-square foot sail gives heavyweights a power edge in strong winds and lightweights a similar edge in lighter airs. Harnesses are disallowed in Olympic competition, requiring supreme physical fitness from all competitors. Further, the Windglider's stiff aluminum mast, fiberglass skinning, mylar sail, and high-mass daggerboard necessitate thoughtful pre-race tuning. Carelessness or misjudgement invite critical losses in positions and points.

Prospects for future Olympics point to a boardsailing "formula," such as those of other yachting classes in which a specified length/width/weight ratio can be met by any qualified manufacturer. Scott approves, stating that he looks forward to competing on the wonderful equipment of the professional World Cup class, but talking with a wistful twinkle of those bright-eyed athletes who'll compete man-against-man in future Olympic formulas.

BREAKING THE SPEED BARRIER: A HARDWARE HAND-OFF

Sequence film clip shows sailor Fred Haywood establishing the world sailboard speed record in Weymouth, England. Streamlined 8' 6" board is a surfsailing outgrowth of Mike Waltze design, incorporating double hard chine rails, double concave bottom shape and ultra-light total weight. Full batten high aspect sail is supported by a high-tech "wing" mast of extreme stiffness, adjustable angle of attack and a weight of only eight pounds. Haywood's record was bettered in 1985 by Michael Pucher at 32.35 knots in France.

As though racing for heaven on a monotone stretch of blue-grey water, surfsailor Fred Haywood used prodigious skill and scientific equipment to exceed 30-knots of speed on a sailboard!

The feat was recorded in October, 1983 at Weymouth, England. Today at this very moment, equipment is being designed to surpass this record. For not only are the builders of Haywood's board and components preparing new equipment to set further records, but others are mounting competitive attempts. The bold quest to meet an "unreachable" goal, when successful, fires the ambitions of barrier breakers.

An effort of this kind is cooperative; creative thinkers conceive the notion, engineers design the equipment, scientists test the engineers, craftsmen fashion the hardware, and an athlete drives the machine. Which single participant is most important? There is an argument for every answer. But the fact is, a sailboard speed record is set both on the drawing board and on the race course. And in this arena it is an axiom that the competition be *unequal*.

ANATOMY OF A RECORD ATTEMPT

Over fifty specialists contributed to the 1983 world sailboard speed record. These included brilliant sailmakers and board builders, ex-

pert designers of components such as booms and mast-to-board couplings, inventive materials suppliers, and—importantly—superior idea people. Tall among these was the chief designer of a revolutionary sailboard "wing" mast, a piercing-eyed man named Dimitrije Milovich. An idea, a plan, an impetus, dedication, excellence, and originality. The ingredients of a superior accomplishment.

Whereas the original basis of sailboard racing was to pit contestant against contestant on like boards and sails, the essence of speed record racing is teamwork; to meet the objective at all odds and all costs. As such, the competition is more than a match of talents; it is also a match of money and management.

CONSUMER TRICKLE-DOWN

Clearly, speed record competition is a highly exclusive form of sailboard racing, requiring funds and technologies that would turn away 99.9% of all competitors. But paradoxically, the fruits of such trail blazing are design and production techniques that are later applied to equipment that mainstream boardsailors can buy and use. These advances, enabling diversification and growth in the sport, make for controversial and exciting prospects for all.

Pivoting with effortless motion and cat-like steps, she faces the spectators with a bright white smile, body angled forward and arms in reverse extention—grasping the boom with her right hand the mast with her left. A sinuous profile against a colorful sail.

Smoothly, with a magician's quickness and the rhythm of a dancer, she steps to the left in an arching twirl, separating herself from sail and rig for what seems like tenths of seconds. With growing intensity and increasing precision, she stabilizes her footing and moves her hands in a fury, spinning the sail in a 360-degree circle!

As if this weren't enough, she then lowers herself yoga-like into a slow motion leg stretch, culminating in a classic ''splits'' position with back fully arched and hair grazing the water. This is *freestyle*, boardsailing in its most graceful splendor.

AN EXPERIMENTAL ART

For many boardsailors, it was just so much splashing around. Nutty stunts and bail-outs after a day of disciplined racing or a full day's work. Messing around with board and sail, trying things out to see what would happen. What evolved was a wonderful ''sport-within-a-sport,'' something impressive to watch and a very real challenge for even the best of sailors to master.

Freestyle is boardsailing in its most personal mode; no one sailor does any one maneuver quite the same as another, and the deveopment of tricks and multi-trick routines is under constant modification and advancement. Unlike traditional figure skating or high diving, where the same essential elements of repertoire have been practiced for decades, freestyle boardsailing is in its infancy; competition events unveil creative new moves almost weekly throughout the world.

It all began with an irreverent disdain for failure. Young sailors such as Matt Schweitzer, well known son of Windsurfing's originator, stretched the limits of their sailboards with inventiveness and skill. An "I can do that" attitude caused bruises on the body and wipeouts in multiples, but it brought about feats unimagined in boardsailing. As these "hotdoggers" exchanged techniques and ideas, names for their maneuvers were established and competitions were staged, comparing one sailor's bag of stunts with another's. What was once laughs and thrills gradually became athletic artistry.

MEASURING EXCELLENCE

Freestyle development and popularity has been fueled by competition. In the early 1980's, compulsory skills and an international scoring system for freestyle were established, enabling equal comparison among sailors. Such systems, although providing a viable measuring device, still carry a large element of the subjective; the opinions of competition judges often vary widely. What's more, it's common for spectators to judge a field of freestylists much differently

than the judges themselves. Excellence is visible, but tough to score.

Today, competitive freestylists are judged in five categories: 1) the number of separate tricks or exercises in a repertoire, 2) the technical difficulty of each trick performed, 3) the style exhibited in the performance of individual exercises, 4) originality of a repertoire, 5) and overall artistic style of the repertoire.

Needless to say, one cannot just sign up and enter a freestyle contest. Sailors must qualify. To do so, generally months—often more than a year of practice is necessary. Contestants in even the smallest events can do a wide range of tricks, have a timed and organized routine or repertoire, and sometimes even exhibit a "theme" in their performances. But freestyle is fun and it's the *getting there* that's so satisfying. Sailing and improving, day-by-day, month-by-month.

LEARNING THE BASICS

Most freestylists are highly skilled basic boardsailors; they can fast tack, power jibe, and execute other such maneuvers as second nature even before stepping up to freestyle. Clearly, it's beneficial to have some advanced basics under your belt before attempting freestyle moves, but U.S.A. Olympic silver medalist Ann Gardner Nelson stresses enthusiasm over skill: "you have to keep trying a trick until you can do it," she advises. Freestyle isn't a breeze for anybody.

At this writing there are at least fifty well established freestyle tricks, ten of which are considered compulsory in competition. For the beginning freestylist, at least five of these exercises, when mastered, will pave the way to learning more advanced skills. These are: 1) the *fast tack* (see page 134), 2) the fast or "*running*" *jibe* (see page 136), 3) the

power jibe (see page 136), 4) the *water start* (see page 133), 5) and the *board* 360.

All of the above basic maneuvers are familiar to experienced regatta sailors; they require a disciplined dexterity which when achieved lays a foundation for advancement. Among competitors, twelve additional exercises are categorized as "basic." They are: *head dip, body dip, stern first, clew first, inside the windward boom, inside the leeward boom, leeward side, back-to-sail, sail 360, sitting, lying, rail ride,* and *tail sink.* Mastering just one of these tricks well is more valuable than repeated "three quarter attempts" at several of them. Excellence achieved in one maneuver breeds "what it takes" to achieve excellence in another.

TO BEGIN

Preparation and equipment for freestyle sailing is essentially the same as for general boardsailing, with particular emphasis on a handful of items. A typical board used should be lengthy, flat, and maneuverable, incorporating "full" rails and a mast foot which cannot accidentally disattach from the board. The board deck and rails should be non-slip coated with sticky parafin wax. For sailors who rail ride, even the daggerboard should be waxed because an anchor foot must be placed on the daggerboard to aid balance.

Ideal wind conditions for freestyle beginners are 3 to 5-knots; proper sail choice is critical here, so as to be neither under or overpowered. Skilled freestylists require stronger winds to execute their more advanced exercises. A battenless sail with a high clew is recommendable.

Physical fitness is especially important, particularly muscle tone. Expert freestylist Ann Gardner Nelson does a full series of grad-

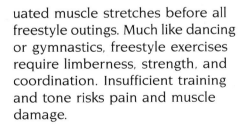

uated muscle stretches before all freestyle outings. Much like dancing or gymnastics, freestyle exercises require limberness, strength, and coordination. Insufficient training and tone risks pain and muscle damage.

BEAUTY IN MOTION

On these pages, champion freestylist Ann Gardner Nelson demonstrates a selection of freestyle exercises that has gained her worldwide recognition and praise. In the sequences that follow, Ann demonstrates some important basic maneuvers and how they're done.

Pre-sailing exercises are essential for freestyle physical conditioning.

"Pirouette"

"Leg Lift"

"Half Splits"

"Clue-first Ballet"

"Clue-first Splits"

"Back-to-Sail, Inside-the-Boom"

"Back-to-Sail, Face-to-Wind"

"Daggerboard Lunge"

"Feet Sailing"

Here, freestyle champion Ann Gardner Nelson demonstrates six maneuvers for the beginning freestylist. While clearly requiring skill and practice, these skills can be accomplished without special physical training such as that required for "splits" and other advanced maneuvers.

Far Left: "Tail sink" or "wheelie" requires steadiness and balance.
Left Page (middle sequence): "Clew first" maneuver incorporates a 180-degree transfer of sail position, requiring rhythm and timing.
Below: "Duck tack" necessitates bringing the sail over the head to change tacks instead of stepping around the front of the mast.
Bottom: "Rail ride" is accomplished by

flipping the board on its rail with both feet and establishing footing on the daggerboard for balance.
Top Right: "Front-to-back" is characterized by standing on the leeward side of sail, facing the sail and holding the boom.
Bottom Right: "Back leg lunge" is a dance-like display stance, used in "transition from trick to trick."

FREESTYLE BASICS WITH ANN GARDNER NELSON

12 TRANSPORT & CARE

*T*he wonderful thing about sailboards is that they're convenient. You can just take them where you please and go sailing. Simple as that. There's one hitch, of course; and it's that you must have a vehicle with which to transport the board and rig! Fortunately, most any vehicle will do.

It is a thankful convenience that no special automobiles or trucks are necessary to carry sailboards to their destinations. Most folks carry their boards efficiently atop their cars on simple rack devices. Generally, only convertibles pose any problem with this method.

RACK TYPES

Most sailboard dealers can supply a wide variety of rack systems. These run from easy-on-and-off "soft" racks (probably not the best choice for freeway driving), to lockable modular systems capable of carrying boards, rigs, bikes, kayaks, skis, and other sports toys. Careful selection of a rack system which is compatible with your car and your equipment will pay off in trouble free (and anxiety free) transportation.

Soft racks consist of a strap arrangement in which cylindrical foam pads encircle durable straps that hook-attach to your automobile rain gutters. These protect both board and cartop, however lack the rigidity of metal racks. But the price is right, and for short junkets they're suprisingly effective.

"Stiff" or metal racks come in several varieties. Usually the base price of these seems quite reasonable, however what you find is that the specific fittings necessary to suit your personal needs can make the dollar tally climb quickly. Even so, these racks are in most cases worth the price. Some things to consider when shopping are: 1) basic sturdiness, 2) mounting convenience, 3) whether or not you desire a locking system, 4) roof-mount compatibility with your car, 5) versatility, 6) and comparative price. Also be sure that any accessories you want for the rack are available and not "on backorder with the distributor."

GETTING THERE

There are various ways to secure and carry equipment on car racks. Although many sailors prefer to completely rig and de-rig before and after each sail (carrying only the bare mast and boom on top of the car with the board) most seem to prefer rolling the sail from the clew toward the mast. Then, leaving the booms attached, the entire rig is put into a zippered

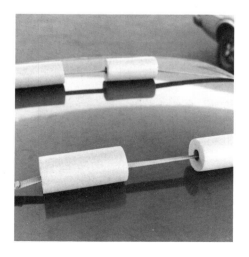

"rig bag" and can be neatly transported. A variation of this method is to detach the booms and roll the sail around the mast, covering it with a long "sail/mast" bag.

In any case, once the racks are installed on the car, both board and rig can be secured by a system of straps—or by the old-fashioned rope tie-down method. Consult the rack maker's instructions and your dealer on this. Generally, strap systems are much preferable to rope, however if you do use rope

or an alternate substitute, be sure to avoid stretchy material such as clothesline or bungee-cord.

OTHER DEVICES

Although uncommon, some boardsailors trailer their boards and rigs. Small, lightweight custom trailers avoid the precarious circumstance of balancing three or four boards plus rigs on a small import coupe or sports car. And they're a solution for the die-hard convertible owner.

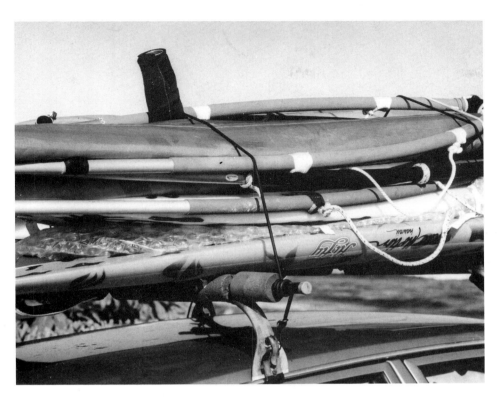

Those who sail frequently at beaches where there is a considerable distance from the parking lot to the water, or who live within walking or bicycling distance of the shore often utilize sand dollies or bicycle trailers. Such devices, while easily home fashioned, are advertised in the sailboard magazines and can sometimes be purchased at sailboard dealers.

Top: Boards and rigs can be secured with straps, rope, or bungee cords (pictured). However, straps are strongly recommended, as rope is less hassle-free and bungees offer less security due to their stretchability.
Top Left: Modern rack systems exhibit superior strength, lightness, and compact design. They're worth the money.
Bottom Far Left: "Soft" racks are inexpensive and effective, however are not recommended for extended freeway driving.

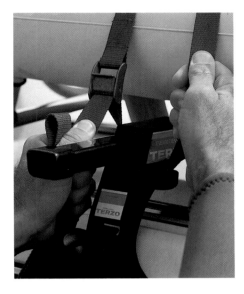

While sailboards can be transported easily on a wide range of vehicles and rack devices, some set-ups are more convenient than others. Here, popular Subaru 4wd station wagon is being fitted with well known adjustable rack system. Racks, board, boom, and mast are mounted and secured in less than seven minutes. Rack system shown can carry one or two boards comfortably, additional boards and rigs with added rack security components. (Automobile provided by Subaru of Southern California, sponsors of sailboard events and supporters of U.S. boardsailing.)

SAILBOARD EQUIPMENT CARE

Boardsailing requires minimal equipment maintenance and very few chores. The boards and rigs of reputable manufacturers, although not indestructable, are easy to take care of and very seldom need replacement parts unless abused. As mentioned in chapter 2, modern boards are constructed largely from urethane foam ''blanks'' which are skinned with a variety of super-durable plastics. Chiefly, these are Polyethylene, ABS, ASA, Epoxy, and polyester/fiberglass.

WASHING THE BOARD

Common domestic liquid kitchen cleaners are effective for this. Heavy tar and other such stains can usually be handled with alcohol or mineral spirits, but be very careful with chemicals such as laquer thinner, acetone, and gasoline; if used on the wrong substance you may risk damage to the skin of your board.

CLEANING THE SAIL

As explained in chapter 4, this is a matter of simple washing, usually with a sponge and hose. If the sail is really soiled, an over-night soak in a freshwater tub with a light detergent is helpful. Follow this with a gentle scrub, using a soft-bristled brush, then rinse in plain water. If a stronger chemical such as acetone or thinner seems to be needed, consult your dealer or sailmaker so as to avoid any possible fiber or color damage.

STORAGE

Be a bit careful here. Because a board can warp, it's best to lay it flat and store it with good support at points along its full length. Sails should be folded or rolled and stored without anything on top of them so as to prevent creasing. Both board and sail should be kept in a clean place.

SAILBOARD REPAIR

Among the booklets and manuals available on sailboard repair (some of them quite good), none seem to address two items: 1) time necessary to accomplish a repair, 2) chemical spillage on clothes and hands, i.e., dealing with a sticky mess! Not to mention the mistakes that usually precede any success. As such, it is recommended here that anything other than minor repairs should be handled by a qualified sailboard shop or suitable craftsman. Further, due to the different chemical properties in the skins of different types of boards, the repair technique on one board may be quite different than that of another.

POLYETHYLENE SKINNING

This material can be heated and melted back together. A soldering iron or hot knife is recommendable for the heating procedure. Cracks, holes, splits, or abrasions can be filled using polyethylene rod or chips. Polyethylene is the softest and simplest sailboard material to work with, with the exception of ''cross linked'' polyethylene. Leave this one to the professionals.

ABS SKINNING

Small ''dings'' in ABS can be repaired by placing a piece (or pieces) of ABS material on the damaged area and melting it with a few drops of acetone. The acetone makes the ABS gummy, after which it can be molded with a soft squeegee. Some dealers carry an ABS solvent paste which accomplishes essentially the same thing as melting pieces into place with acetone. It's a little quicker and neater.

ASA SKINNING

The ABS repair procedure also works with ASA, however some ASA composites have been known to discolor when melted. It's advisable to consult your dealer here.

EPOXY SKINNING

Two repair methods are effective with epoxy skins; the ABS method and also through using an epoxy resin with a hardening catalyst. Epoxy resins can generally be purchased at marine hardware stores; a slow-setting resin is advisable because it functions with limited heat expansion and gives you more time to work on the repair before it ''sets up.''

FIBERGLASS SKINNNG

This requires a polyester resin, hardening catalyst, and either fiberglass cloth or matte to re-skin the damaged area. The repair procedure is not unlike that of using familiar two-tube epoxy glues, except that polyester resin has less viscosity, somewhat comparable to 50-weight oil. Care must be taken to purchase a ''finishing resin'' that hardens and can be sanded. Interim step ''glassing resins'' dry tacky instead of fully cured.

UNDER-SKIN REPAIRS

Sailboard cores are predominantly made from polyurethane foam. If board damage is so severe that the core is injured, a ''pie-cut'' can be taken from the board and replaced with an entirely new piece of foam. Using a file and sandpaper, the new piece of foam can be contoured to the rest of the board and then covered with the appropriate skinning. An exception to this is the rare but increasingly prevalent polystyrene foam core, generally associated with epoxy boards. Whereas polyurethane foam is retardent to water seepage, polystyrene is sponge-like in its absorption of water if damaged, discouraging piece-fit repairs.

OTHER REPAIRS

Aside from board damage, the most common problems are daggerboard, skeg, and mast breakages. Because skegs and daggerboards are relatively inexpensive, it is simple and advisable to replace them if broken. Masts, however, can be repaired through splinting and wrapping techniques which if accomplished properly are quite satisfactory. Consult your dealer for details pertaining to your mast type.

Wetsuits, drysuits, and booties—those treasured boardsailor's vitals—can develop tears or splits from rigorous use. Replacing a quality wetsuit or drysuit is expensive and is generally unnecessary unless the suit is rotted, completely worn out, or badly mangled. Most sailors repair them. Traditional ''wetsuit glue'' can be purchased at scuba diving shops, however most sailboard dealers recommend an excellent product, ''Aquaseal.'' This is a clear, gluey substance that comes in a tube, is easy to apply, and melds rubber substances together sensationally. When dry, Aquaseal is flexible just like rubber.

13 BOARDSAILING THROUGH THE LENS

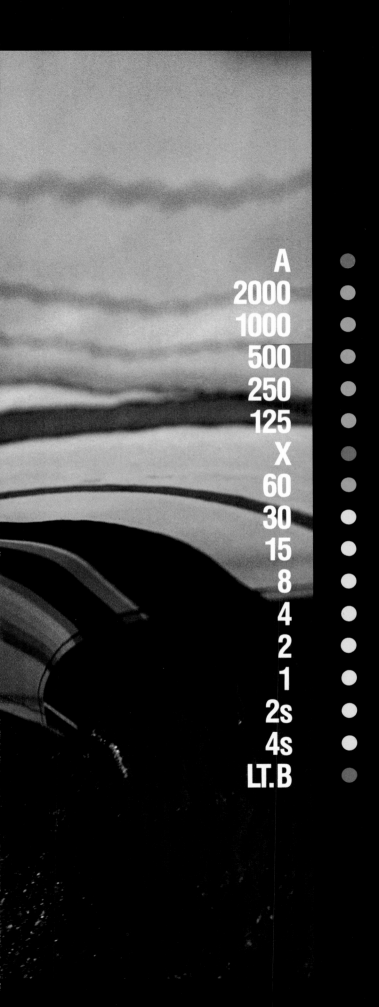

A
2000
1000
500
250
125
X
60
30
15
8
4
2
1
2s
4s
LT.B

*N*o matter where you go board-sailing, whether it's bouncing over the moguls at Diamond Head, sailing a one-design race in San Diego, or perfecting a freestyle maneuver off Antigua, you'll find cameras. Photography and the sport of boardsailing are such natural compliments to each other that it's almost impossible to separate them. The beauty, grace and power of boardsailing are wonderful to capture. Your camera is the consumate tool for preserving the experiences and beauty of the sport.

For many boardsailors, packing a camera when going to the beach is as natural as bringing a harness or high-wind sail. The camera is a prized accessory and, fortunately, a boardsailing photographer doesn't need to spend years studying the nuances of photography to get good pictures. Nor is it necessary to take an advanced course in camera repair to keep your camera working in hostile marine environments. You just have to understand the equipment and a few simple rules. It helps to be willing to look at board-sailing photography as a learning experi-ence, just like boardsailing itself. If you are willing to take some time—to practice and not be disappointed by less than perfect results —your photography will improve steadily.

EQUIPMENT

YOUR CAMERA

To a great extent, the results of your photographic efforts will be dictated by your choice of equipment. Now this doesn't mean you have to own a professional camera "system" with a dozen lenses and a 6-frame-per-second motor drive! But to capture the drama of boardsailing you'll need something more sophisticated than an "instamatic." A medium-priced 35mm single-lens-reflex (SLR) with through-the-lens metering is ideal. The modern 35mm SLR is relatively inexpensive, can be fitted with a wide variety of lenses and other accessories and is easily handled.

Smaller "pocket" cameras, though good for snapshots, don't offer interchangable lenses, thus make it difficult to focus in close on your subject. Further, small 110 film sizes usually prohibit really good enlargements. Larger format cameras, such as the Hassleblad, Bronica, & Mamiya 645, are of high quality and offer a wide variety of accessories. They feature a large film size which enables super enlargements. But for the average sailor/photographer, these cameras are very expensive and somewhat demanding to operate.

If you already own a good 35mm SLR, great. If you don't, and you're serious about taking pictures, it's advisable to buy one. The cost is less than a new custom sail, and will last a lot longer! When you go to the camera store, look at more than just the camera itself; analyze the system that backs it up. Are there a wide variety of lenses available? Can it be fitted with a power winder? If you are buying a camera in the middle of a manufacturer's line and you think you might want to upgrade at a later date, be sure the lenses and other accessories you buy will adapt to the higher priced camera. Also consider the reputation of the manufacturer. Talk to people you know and ask their opinions, but don't let them set your mind unless you know their work and respect their judgement. It is best not to go to the camera store with a preconceived idea of which camera to buy. Talk to one or two salespeople, hold the cameras and get the feel of them. A camera is a very personal piece of equipment. Like a custom sailboard— get the one that feels right to you, one that you're comfortable with.

LENSES

Once you have the camera, you'll need a couple of lenses to get your picture taking underway. But before choosing them, it's important to know something about the characteristics of various types of lenses. There's nothing worse than plunking down money because a salesperson said "you have to have this" and then finding that it doesn't suit your needs. So bear with us a minute for some "optical talk."

There are two terms important in discussing lenses. The first is "lens speed." All lenses are rated for their speed; this is given as an "f-number." This number corresponds to the widest aperture opening of a particular lens, or how much light the lens is physically able to collect. The smaller the

f-number, the faster the lens. The second term is "depth of field." This refers to the area of the photograph that is in acceptable focus. With all lenses, when you focus on a subject there is an area both in front of and behind your subject that is out of focus. Faster lenses have greater depth of field, allowing for focus in a greater area both in front of and behind your subject. They give you more "focus latitude."

The "normal" lens that comes with your camera will probably be either a 50mm or 55mm. This lens will give an image approximately the same as that seen through the naked eye. Normal lenses are usually "fast," in the f/1.2 to f/2 range. They are practically free of distortion and have a very acceptable depth-of-field. Normal lenses are ideal for shooting around the beach and for taking seascapes. With their speed, lack of distortion, and depth-of-field, they are the easiest of lenses to use. Unfortunately normal lenses are often too short to take photos of boardsailing on the water —but don't discount them. Their versatility is always surprising.

Wide-angle lenses, which range in focal length from the fisheye to approximately 35mm are a wonderful but often overlooked addition to the boardsailing photographer's arsenal. While not recommended as a first lens, a good wide-angle is a great second or third purchase. Wide-angles are usually slightly slower than normal lenses; f/2.4 and f/3.5 being common, but they take in a vast amount of scenery and collect more than enough light for use in beach photography. These lenses also have great depth-of-field, making them perfect for snapshots on the beach. Their particular characteristics, stretched perspective and great depth-of-field, can be used to create spectacular effects.

TELEPHOTO TECHNIQUE

When people think of boardsailing photography, they usually think of rows of mega-millimeter lenses mounted on sturdy tripods arranged on the hill above Hookipa or aimed at the speeding course racers of Kailua Bay. Therefore, when a professional first contemplates boardsailing photography, the long lens is the first purchase, and rightly so. In most cases the only way to capture the action of boardsailing is with a telephoto. Long lenses, like short lenses, have their own peculiarities which are important to understand. The longer the lens, the less depth-of-field. This makes focus critical; in many instances the area of acceptable focus will be far less than the length of a board. The longer a lens is, the more it compresses perspective, or flattens the depth of a photograph, pushing the subject in the foreground against the background. There is nothing you can do to change these idiosyncracies; becoming familiar with them will help you take good pictures with your long lens.

Two other characteristics of long lenses are of critical import-ance. The first is the speed of the lens. Long lenses tend to be slow. If you buy one that's too slow, it will either force you to use only high speed film, or dictate shooting at such slow shutter speeds that you're unable to stop action. Most sailboarding takes place in bright sunlight, but even on the brightest of days, a lens with a speed of, say, f/6.8 can be too slow to allow you to shoot at a high shutter speed. When seeking a long lens, spend the extra money and buy a fast one, at least an f/4 or f/4.5.

The second factor important to long lens use is the focal length

itself. All lenses are subject to your physical body movement when you take a picture. The longer the lens the tougher it is to hold the camera still. Most people feel the longest lens you can successfully hand-hold is 400mm. To do that, you have to shoot at least 1/500th of a second and brace your elbows against your body. Anything longer than a 400 is tough to use without a tripod.

ZOOM LENSES

"Zoom" lenses allow for a wide variety of focal lengths without the bother of changing lenses. This also reduces the expense of purchasing several different lenses. Zooms are a good bet for boardsailing photography but have some limitations. Like long telephotos, zooms tend to be somewhat slow lenses, and due to their optical complexities inexpensive zoom lenses lack the sharpness of fixed lenses. It is human nature to contemplate saving money when you look at two lenses that appear very similar, but if you buy a slow lens that is not sharp, little is achieved. In zooms, more than any other lenses, you get what you pay for. So do your homework in the camera consumer reports if you desire a decent zoom lens.

It's prudent to buy either an ultra violet (UV) or skylight filter immediately. The filter will protect the delicate coating on the front of the lens element from spray and grit. It also will cut the overall blue tint you get when shooting around the water, yet won't affect the speed of the lens.

USEFUL ACCESSORIES

For the boardsailing photographer, a power winder or a motor drive is effective and exciting to use. Picture taking becomes faster

and easier. And a lot more action can be captured. But look out! The film will fly! Winders and motors are far from necessity. There is no substitute for skilled timing, the ability to shoot at the precise instant necessary to capture the image you want. Rapid shooting is fun, but disciplined shooting produces the results.

Lens filters can be useful accessories. If shooting color film, you might want to try a polarizing filter; this will cut glare and deepen color saturation. However, this filter may force you to use a faster film. Faster film means more ''grain'' in your images. If you are shooting black and white, a yellow filter increases the contrast between whites and blues, giving you a darker sky and whiter clouds. A red filter will exaggerate this effect. There are a wide variety of special effects filters available for use with both black and white and color film, and you might enjoy experimenting. Any of these filters can be used with the UV or skylight filter left in place.

FILM

Shooting good photos requires a solid foundation in equipment and film. A foundation you can know and trust. Careless applica-tion of equipment or film will yield little. The largest and most controllable variable is film. It is best to look at the films available, select the one that suits your needs, and stick with it. A quick stop at the drug store enroute to the beach invites buying whatever happens to be on the shelf. Inferior or unfamiliar film is the bain of even the best photographers. Standard-izing on a specific film will speed your progress, enabling consistency and analysis.

Most professional surfing and marine photographers use Koda-chrome 64. This film is extremely fine-grained and gives excellent color rendition: bright blue skies, clean whites and yellows, and bright greens and reds. Its ASA speed of 64 allows you to shoot in marginal light situations at high shutter speeds and still get some depth-of-field with your long lens. If you prefer color prints, both Kodacolor and Fujicolor offer fine grain, sharpness, and good color print reproduction. For spectacular black and white, Ilford XP1 offers wide film speed flexibility and superior tonal quality. Kodak's black and white film types are also excellent.

For action, most pros have learned through experience to shoot at a minimum of 1/500th of a second. This is fast enough to stop the action on the water, yet still give a reasonable f-stop for depth-of-field and sharp-ness. By sticking with the same film and shutter speed, you will eliminate most of your in-camera variables. Not only will you be able to more accurately judge your progress, but it will also get you used to seeing the same numbers coming up in your light meter. Experiments with slow shutter speeds, strobes and other variables can yield fascinating results, but until your basic skills are developed, much film will be wasted!

READING LIGHT

Becoming familiar with what your meter should be reading is very important around the water. Often, your meter will trick you. Light reflecting off the water, a wet mylar sail, the sand, or even the white foam of a breaking wave can con-found a light meter. If, by using the same film and shutter speed com-bination, you get used to seeing the same f-stop appearing under the same conditions, you will learn to compensate for your meter. If you've been shooting at f/5.6 and your meter suddenly snaps up to f/22, take a second to really look through your viewfinder. Not just at the subject you've been focus-ing on, but the whole area. Have you swung so that you're facing the sun? Has the background changed significantly? It's not impossible to take pictures in these difficult lighting situations; it just takes practice.

The time of day you shoot is nearly as important as what you shoot. Careful photographers avoid the middle of the day when the sun is brightest. Best results come early or late in the day when the sun is slanting across the water. This enables dramatic front-lit and back-lit photos.

BRACKETING

"Bracketing" is shooting with both larger and smaller aperature openings than your light meter specifically dictates. This gives you the photo you want in more than one exposure, allowing darker and lighter versions of the same subject.

For consistent good results, it's highly advisable to bracket. All pros do.

If you are focusing on a wet mylar sail, your meter may jump three or four stops because of the intense reflected light produced from the sail. The natural reaction when this happens is to close down the aperature so as to limit such extreme light. But your meter is tricking you; it's not reading the light on the sail as you would like to see the sail. It is reacting to the tremendous reflection from the sail. Bracketing will help you learn to get good results in situations like this.

SPECIAL TOOLS FOR THE WET AND WILD

So you want to get in the water and try your luck at the dramatic stuff. Well, this is a subject for at

CAMERA TECHNIQUE

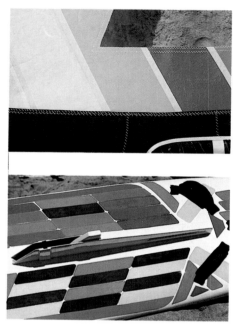

Boardsailing photography can be action, beauty, art, fun—whatever the photographer desires. Here, impulse snapshots, patient "set-ups," and risky water shots sit side-by-side, for beauty is in the eye of the picture-maker.

GET INTO ACTION

least one complete book, however here are a few pointers. The celebrated Nikonos, best known all around 35mm water camera, can be handled by most amateurs. However the Nikonos—and its small handful of alternatives—require some money. Here, you're edging that realm of special equipment. With special equipment comes extra expenditure. Further, most skilled boardsailing and marine photographers use their regular equipment, protecting it with sophisticated water cases. These cases, often custom made to specification, require careful technique to use effectively and must be disassembled for film reloading. And each lens necessitates a specially sized plexiglass front muzzle for the case to accommodate it. Conventional "water" cameras such as the Nikonos do not accommodate winders and have limited lens options.

The "soft case" is the most accessible means by which to actually get into the water and take pictures. Retailing for generally less than $100, this is an ingenious device that houses your camera (with winder if desired), and can accommodate the "shorter" lenses—roughly 20mm through 85mm. The case, actually a plasticized sack that incorporates an inner glove for your hand, can yield a wide variety of great results but won't house a long telephoto. Water work with a telephoto requires a professional

hard case and a fair sized wallet. And beware, any kind of water work risks leakage and equipment damage. All photographers are on their own in the "aqua frontier."

THE VIEWER'S WORLD

Here is a wonderful place. With a telephoto lens you can "scope in" on a colorful sail, catch the transparent beauty from "back-lit" sunlight. With a wide angle lens you can shoot low and close to a competitor tuning his rig, creating a feeling of dimension and a pre-race urgency. With an auto-winder you can follow a fast moving wave sailor, capturing every turn and cutback on a single roll of film. What you see through the viewfinder can be yours for all time!

But you must concentrate. And you must analyze. While the human eye is selective, the camera's lens is not. When you look through the viewfinder, you see your subject, focus in, and fire! What you end up with when slides or prints come back may be something different from what you thought you saw. Unless you examine the entire contents of the frame, you may find yourself shooting backgrounds and other oddities that at first glance go unnoticed. But though unnoticed, your trusty SLR records all. Beware of power lines, tree tops, smoke stacks, and the like. It takes attentiveness and care to really shoot what you really see.

It was the world famous photographer Henri Cartier Bresson who became known for recording "the decisive moment" in a scene or action. In boardsailing, the decisive moment is paramount. While matters of composition, angle, and color are best left to personal judgement, split second timing can make or break almost any boardsailing photograph. True masters of the subject

vary greatly in their equipment and styles. But they would all agree: you gotta be there, you gotta be in position, and you gotta get it while it's happening. No excuses. The pictures won't record what might have been. And what a great feeling to be on top of the action, focused in and fully loaded with film! Get out there and do it. Talk is cheap. And so is film. The decisive moment is priceless.

You don't have to keep your camera equipment so protected or so antiseptic as to panic if a single drop of water or grain of sand finds its way onto a lens or camera body. All that's necessary is to care for photo gear just as for any finely crafted tool. Periodic cleaning and good user habits are sufficient. A padded, water repellant camera bag will start you on the foot here. This will give you a protective storage place for camera, lenses, film, spare batteries, and miscellaneous.

In your camera bag, safely protected in a plastic bag, keep a cleaning kit. All that's needed is a bottle of lens cleaning solution, a pad of lens tissue, a "blower" aerosol or brush, and cotton swabs. A chamois cloth is an ideal "camera wiper" and a pencil eraser is effective for cleaning battery and electrical terminals. Your kit may grow as you find items needed for your particular camera model and system, but this is a good start.

LENS CARE

When shooting, the most exposed (thus most vulnerable) component is the camera lens. While the front element is exposed to wind-driven spray and sand, the focusing ring, f/stop ring, and—if the lens is a zoom—the focal length adjusting ring or slide is subject to damage from sand and grit. During lens changing, the rear lens element becomes vulnerable along with the inside of the camera body.

When you bought your lens, you also probably bought either a UV or skylight filter. Once you've cleaned your front element carefully with lens cleaning solution and lint-free lens tissue, screw the filter on and never take it off. Then, when cleaning the front of your lens while shooting, you'll be cleaning the inexpensive filter, not the expensive, delicate front element. If the filter gets scratched it can be discarded and replaced with a new one at a fraction of the cost of a new front element.

Even with a filter in place over the front element, it's a good idea to keep the lens cap on when you're not shooting. This will protect the lens if it gets knocked about.

As for the barrel of the lens and its rings and slides, the best care is prevention. Don't set the lens in the sand, and, whenever possible, shield it from wind-blown sand. After each use, carefully wipe the lens barrel with a clean, dry, lint-free cloth. Your blower brush will be excellent to get around the rings and slides to remove grit.

When bought, your lens came with an end cap, for covering for the rear element. Whenever you take a lens off your camera, be sure to fit the end cap to it. Along with shielding the rear element, the end cap will also provide protection for the mount and the meter coupling. Take a second before you attach the end cap to be sure that it is completely free of sand, grit and moisture.

CAMERA BODY CARE

While the camera's lens is the most vulnerable component, the camera body is by no means invulnerable. Around the water, modern cameras, with their electronics and computer chips, must be cared for more carefully than their predecessors. Cognizant of this, the manufacturers have provided you with various protective pieces for your camera body. These include such items as the hot shoe cover and the caps on your flash sync terminals. These should be left in place to protect electrical contacts from spray. Common sense is the best defense you can use as far as protecting the camera body; try to keep it clean and dry. It will, of course, get spray and grit on it, but try to keep this to a minimum. The same soft towel and blower brush you used on the barrel of your lens can be employed on the camera body to dry and clean it.

The viewfinder eyepiece is a part of the camera body that does require some special attention. Recessed as it is on most cameras, it collects grit and spray. This can get so bad that it's actually hard to see to focus. Clean the eyepiece regularly with a wad of lens tissue or a cotton swab moistened with lens cleaning solution. Be sure to clean gently to avoid scratching the optically-ground glass.

The real danger to your camera comes when the body is opened. This occurs when changing lenses, film or batteries. In each case, the delicate, highly-sophisticated internal workings of your camera will be exposed to a hostile environment. Whenever you have to open your camera body, take just a moment to do some preventative maintenance. It can save costly factory repairs later.

Depending upon conditions, use your cleaning chamois or blower brush to carefully wipe around whichever portion of your camera you are going to open. This will prevent grit from getting into the camera. When you open the camera, be sure to block it from direct wind. As your camera is most vulnerable when it is open, keep it open for as short a time as possible, have the new lens, fresh film, or battery ready. Get them installed and the camera sealed as quickly as possible.

Learning sailboarding photography can be as much fun and as rewarding as learning boardsailing. A natural symbiotic relationship exists between boardsailing and photography, and mastering each discipline adds enjoyment to the other. The suggestions and hints in this chapter should be enough to get you on your way to taking more and better pictures of your boardsailing adventures.

CAMERA CARE NOTES

GLOSSARY

AFT
Toward the rear or tail of the board

APPARENT WIND
The wind felt by the sailor—created by the motion of the board and sail as they move over the water

BACK HAND
The hand closest to the back of the board

BEAM REACH
Sailing with the sail approximately 50 to 60 degrees from the board's centerline—direction of movement will be 90 degrees off the wind

BEAR OFF
To turn the board away from the wind

BEAT
Sailing on an upwind leg of a course

BROAD REACH
Sailing with the sail approximately 70 to 80 degrees from the board's centerline—direction of movement will be about 120 degrees off the wind

CENTERBOARD
Has same function as daggerboard, but can be retracted mechanically

CLEW
Outer, rear corner of the sail. The outhaul attaches at this point

CLOSE HAULED
Sailing as close as possible to the wind—direction of movement will be 45 degrees off the wind

CLOSE REACH
Sailing with the sail approximately 30 degrees from the board's centerline—direction of movement will be about 60 degrees off the wind

COME ABOUT
See Tack

DAGGERBOARD
A wood or plastic board inserted into the hull of a boat or sailboard which provides lateral resistance to slipping sideways in the water

DOWNHAUL
A line which attaches the sail to the universal joint

EYE OF THE WIND
The direction from which the actual wind is blowing

FLOATER
A board with enough flotation to remain floating while stationary

FREESAIL SYSTEM
A sail system that incorporates a universal joint at the base of the mast to allow for movement of the rig in any direction

FRONT HAND
The hand closest to the front of the board

HARNESS
Device which allows sailor to reduce load off of arms by using body weight to counter-balance the force of the wind in the sail

HEAD UP
To turn closer to the eye of the wind

HYPOTHERMIA
A potentially fatal condition where temperature of the body core is lowered from exposure to cold, wet, or wind

IBSA
International Boardsailing Association

IYRU
International Yacht Racing Union

JIBE
A change of board direction in which the stern passes through the eye of the wind

LEECH
The back edge of sail that extends from the head to the clew

LEEWARD
The side of the board wind is blowing with

LUFFING
When the sail is fluttering and not filled with wind, sail and clew are directly into the wind

MAST FOOT
The bottom part of the mast that fits into the mast well or step

OFFSHORE BREEZE
A breeze blowing from the land to the water

OLYMPIC TRIANGLE
A commonly used racing course with three equal legs and 60 degree turns at each mark

ONSHORE BREEZE
A breeze blowing from the water to the land

OUTHAUL
Line which pulls the clew of the sail out to the end of the boom—used to control sail curvature

PORT
The left side of the board when facing forward

PUMPING
Maneuver which creates wind in the sail and gives the board extra speed. IYRU rules allow only three pumps in racing

RAILS
The lengthwise edges of the board

REACH
Sailing with the wind from the side. See beam reach, broad reach, or close reach

R.A.F. SAIL
A "rotating air foil" sail design which incorporates full battens and enables the battens to rotate around the mast from side to side, thus creating a "clean" efficient sail shape.

RIG
Entire sail assembly from the universal up—mast, booms, sail, battens, and universal

SHEET IN
Pulling in with back hand to completely fill sail with wind

SHEET OUT
Letting out with back hand to let wind spill from the sail

SINKER
A type of short board that cannot support the sailor's weight unless sailing. Must be water started

SKEG
Any of the variety of fins that are underneath in the back end of a board

STARBOARD
The right side of the board when facing forward

TACK
1. A change of board direction in which the front of the board moves through the eye of the wind. 2. The inside bottom corner of the sail near the mast foot. 3. Sail to windward on alternating courses

TAIL
The back end of the board

UNIVERSAL JOINT
The joint at the base of the mast that allows for movement of the rig in any direction while connecting the rig to the board

UPHAUL
The line used to pull the rig from the water

WINDWARD
The side closest to the wind

☑ *Yes, I am interested in sailboarding information & accessories.*

Name _____

Address _____

City _____ *State* _____ *Zip* _____

Orders & Information: GrubbStake
Media Ltd., 2906A W. Pacific Coast
Hwy., Newport Beach, CA 92663

Grubbstake Media Ltd.
2906-A W. Pacific Coast Hwy.
Newport Beach, CA 92663